Gardening
With Lunar Lore

Peter West

GREEN MAGIC

Peter West
mrpwest@googlemail.com

Gardening with Lunar Lore © 2020 by PENTAGON.

Green Magic
53 Brooks Road
Street
Somerset
BA16 0PP
England

www.greenmagicpublishing.com

Cover design by
Mark Gotto

Designed and typeset by K.DESIGN
Winscombe, Somerset

ISBN 9781916014015

GREEN MAGIC

Contents

INTRODUCTION

The Gardening Year

THIS REALLY IS a misnomer of a title if ever there was one because, for the ardent gardener, there is no start or finish, it is just one long – very long – period of incessant hard work.

And even if people use astrological knowledge to help them achieve better results it may ease the load somewhat, but the pressure is never really very far away. Admittedly, all this is likely to be swept aside when the results come through.

Beds of colourful flowers, bushes and trees brimming with fruit, their yield a tribute to the time spent nurturing them. Then there are the vegetable growths to be appreciated as row upon row of edible and tasty additions to meals spring forth. And one can pass by lush green lawns to admire while others lounge on garden furniture, perhaps spread around sparkling ponds and rockeries?

Well, that is one view.

There are a few people, not many perhaps, who have a natural gift for gardening. "Green fingers" is the usual term. It denotes those who seem to have only to touch this or dig that and a few weeks later they create perfect results.

Why Astrology and Gardening?

For many centuries, these two disciplines have been inextricably linked. In that farmers, and gardeners have been sowing, planting, cultivating and gathering in their various growths in tune with the signs of the zodiac or, to be more precise, when the Moon is known to have been in this or that sign.

There are those who speak of leaf, flower, root and fruit days and of planting or sowing this or that when the Moon is transiting (passing through) a particular sign. Many are not totally aware of why, because it is the way this knowledge has been passed down through the ages, but with such excellent results.

Through the years, I have found these four basic terms seem to either cloud the issue or make it hard for the ordinary person to understand. I will explain them so that you may experiment, but I prefer 'when and where' to do 'what and when' as the Moon passes through 'this or that' sign and, most importantly, what phase she is in at that time.

Leaf days are when the Moon is transiting or passing through Cancer, Scorpio or Pisces, also known as the Water signs. It is suggested that these are the best times to plant out or sow vegetables like cabbage, lettuce or other plants noted for their leaf foods.

Flower days are when the Moon is in Aries, Leo or Sagittarius, also known as the Fire signs. It has been recommended that these are the best days to sow or plant out cauliflowers, broccoli and so on.

Root days are when the Moon is passing through Taurus, Virgo or Capricorn, also known as the Earth signs. When the Moon is here, one should deal with plants which supply food that grow in the ground like potatoes, parsnips and carrots.

Fruit days are associated with Gemini, Libra or Aquarius, the Air signs, and it is suggested these times are when you should concentrate on planting or sowing tomatoes, peas and beans.

A more complete understanding of what exercise to pursue at any given time is explained in the chapter called Astrological Lunar Lore.

In the Lunar Activity Guide you will find all the usual plants we might normally associate with gardening, along with the best times for when and how you should pursue such things.

Now you can join that happy band of people simply by observing the astrological hints given for each month. However, you must also try to remember that the weather indicators are usually presented in, or have to be, in a widely general form. There is rarely enough space to localise this information. For those seriously interested there are books available that specialise in weather forecasting using lunar and planetary lore.

However, let us return to gardening lunar lore. Please note that all vegetables, fruits and plants mentioned for one activity or another throughout this book are referred to as their most astrologically appropriate lunar time and sign for the reader to plant or sow.

You are also reminded that, up until now, you would have been asked to use a good gardening guide for the proper season and best month in which to actually start the plant or growths concerned. As much information as possible has been has been included in the relevant chapter in respect of the month concerned, and you will also find that you can cross reference these exercises with other plants of a similar nature.

A word of caution perhaps might also be helpful at this stage. It is not always possible to follow the advice given in the ensuing pages for one reason or another – especially where the weather is concerned. This is why space has been allowed to outline the average expectations for each month.

A chapter on astrological weather forecasting has been included for, in this country especially, so much depends on what does happen not just in our gardening worlds but also in the greater farming communities as well. Alternative times for many activities have been included for just such occasions.

The work listed here to be undertaken during each month is far from complete because this whole book is meant as a general guide. Where a task is advised that you try to time your efforts with either the phase of the moon or its position to do this or that on a particular day is not complete either.

Because a task or tip has not been mentioned in either category does not mean you should not pursue such work. It simply means it hasn't been included

However, there is one golden rule to observe, even if you are not an astrological gardener. One should never start or try to finish any activity or task under a "void-of-course" (v-o-c) moon for nothing ever goes right at such times.

I have included a complete explanation of what a void-of-course moon is and what to expect when it does happen and this will be found in the chapter on the void-of-course moon.

Happy gardening.

PART ONE

Lunar Garden Activity Guide

THIS CHAPTER CONCERNS itself with the when and how of planting and sowing vegetables, flowers, fruit trees, bushes, herbs, and all other garden growths and activities. Where possible, I have tried to list what I can in respect of everything one might encounter while in the average garden but, as with all things, the list is not complete. Nevertheless, if it isn't mentioned it doesn't mean you cannot undertake the task.

Thus, the majority of plants, vegetables and fruits are listed along with the best period, phase (or quarter) of the Moon. Also shown is the best time for which sign the Moon passes through for such activities. Sometimes, you will find that a sign is suggested that may not agree with the Moon phase of the moment or, vice versa, imply a phase that may seem out of kilter with the sign the Moon occupies.

What is important to you is that all these recommendations have been checked and what is here are the most favoured signs and times for planting or sowing for each month of the gardening year.

For example, as an astrological guide, a good period, although not necessarily for the first time in the year, one should sow broccoli or cauliflower is during the first week of March. The list recommends one should wait for the Moon may be in a position for this or that to be sown or planted a week earlier or later. Be guided accordingly.

FRUIT AND VEGETABLES

PLANT	PHASE	SIGN
Annuals	1 or 2	Libra
Apple tree	3	Taurus, Cancer, Sagittarius, Pisces
Apricot tree	2 or 3	Taurus, Libra, Capricorn
Artichoke (both types)	1	Taurus, Cancer, Virgo, Pisces
Asparagus	1	Cancer, Scorpio, Pisces
Aubergine	2	Cancer, Libra, Scorpio, Pisces
Barley	1 or 2	Cancer, Libra, Capricorn, Pisces
Beans	2	Taurus, Cancer, Libra, Pisces
Beech Tree	2 or 3	Capricorn
Beetroot	3	Cancer, Libra, Scorpio, Capricorn, Pisces
Bramble fruit	2	Cancer, Scorpio, Pisces
Broccoli	1	Cancer, Libra, Scorpio, Pisces
Blackberry	2	Cancer, Scorpio, Pisces
Brussels Sprout	1	Cancer, Libra, Scorpio, Pisces
Bulbs	3	Cancer, Scorpio, Pisces
Bulbs for seed	2 or 3	
Cabbage	1	Taurus, Cancer, Libra, Scorpio, Pisces
Carrot	3	Taurus, Cancer, Libra, Scorpio, Pisces
Cauliflower	1	Cancer, Libra, Scorpio, Pisces

PLANT	PHASE	SIGN
Celeriac	3	Taurus, Cancer, Libra, Scorpio, Pisces
Celery	1	Cancer, Scorpio, Pisces
Cherry tree	2 or 3	Taurus, Libra, Capricorn
Chicory	2 or 3	Cancer, Scorpio, Pisces
Clover	1 or 2	Cancer, Scorpio, Pisces
Corn	1	Cancer, Scorpio, Pisces
Courgettes	2	Cancer, Libra, Scorpio, Pisces
Cress	1	Cancer, Scorpio, Pisces
Cucumber	1	Cancer, Scorpio, Pisces
Deciduous trees	2 or 3	Cancer, Virgo, Libra, Scorpio, Pisces
Eggplant	2	Cancer, Libra, Scorpio, Pisces
Endive	1	Cancer, Scorpio, Pisces, Gemini, Libra, Aquarius
Evergreen trees	2 or 3	Cancer, Virgo, Libra, Scorpio, Pisces
Fig tree	2 or 3	Taurus, Libra
Flowers	1 or 2	Taurus, Cancer, Virgo, Libra,
	1 or 2	Scorpio, Pisces
Garlic	1 or 2	Scorpio, Sagittarius
Gooseberry	2	Cancer, Scorpio, Pisces
Grape	2 or 3	Taurus, Cancer, Virgo, Scorpio, Pisces
Herbs	1 or 2	Cancer, Scorpio, Pisces
Horseradish	1 or 2	Virgo, Scorpio
Houseplants	1	Cancer, Scorpio, Pisces
Kohlrabi	1 or 2	Cancer, Libra, Scorpio, Pisces
Lawns	4	Virgo, Leo, Gemini

PLANT	PHASE	SIGN
Leek	2 or 3	Sagittarius
Lettuce	1	Taurus, Cancer, Libra, Scorpio, Pisces
Maple tree	2 or 3	Taurus, Cancer, Virgo, Pisces
Marrow	1 or 2	Cancer, Scorpio, Pisces
Melon	1 or 2	Cancer, Scorpio, Pisces
Mushroom	1 or 2	Cancer
Nectarine tree	2 or 3	Taurus, Virgo, Libra
Nut tree	2 or 3	Cancer, Scorpio, Pisces
Oak tree	3	Sagittarius
Oats	1 or 2	Cancer, Libra, Scorpio, Pisces
Onion (seeds)	2	Libra Scorpio, Sagittarius
Onion (sets)	3 or 4	Taurus, Libra, Pisces
Parsley	1	Cancer, Libra, Scorpio, Pisces
Parsnip	3	Taurus, Cancer, Scorpio, Pisces
Peach tree	2 or 3	Taurus, Virgo, Libra
Pear tree	2 or 3	Taurus, Virgo, Libra
Peas	2	Cancer, Libra, Scorpio, Pisces
Peppers	2	Cancer, Scorpio, Pisces
Plum tree	2 or 3	Taurus, Virgo, Libra
Potatoes	3	Taurus, Cancer, Scorpio, Capricorn
Privet hedge	1 or 2	Taurus, Libra
Pumpkin	2	Cancer, Libra, Scorpio, Pisces
Quince	1 or 2	Capricorn
Radish	3	Taurus, Libra, Capricorn, Pisces
Raspberry	2	Cancer, Scorpio, Pisces
Rhubarb	3	Cancer, Pisces
Sage	3	Cancer, Scorpio, Pisces

PLANT	PHASE	SIGN
Saffron	1 or 2	Cancer, Scorpio, Pisces
Sage	3	Cancer, Scorpio, Pisces
Salsify	1 or 2	Cancer, Scorpio, Pisces
Shallot	2	Scorpio, Sagittarius
Spinach	1	Cancer, Scorpio, Pisces
Strawberry	3	Cancer, Scorpio, Pisces
String Bean	1 or 2	Taurus
Sweet Corn	1	Cancer, Scorpio, Pisces
Sweet Peas	1 or 2	Cancer, Virgo Pisces
Tomato	2	Cancer, Scorpio, Capricorn, Pisces
Trees (shade)	3	Taurus, Capricorn
Trees (ornamental)	2	Taurus, Libra
Tubers (for seed)	3	Cancer, Libra, Scorpio, Pisces
Turnip	3	Taurus, Cancer, Libra, Scorpio, Pisces
Swede	3	Taurus, Cancer, Libra, Scorpio, Pisces
Valerian	1 or 2	Gemini, Virgo
Watercress	1	Cancer, Scorpio, Pisces
Watermelon	1 or 2	Cancer, Libra, Scorpio, Pisces
Wheat	1 or 2	Cancer, Libra, Scorpio, Pisces

FLOWERS

The general consensus of astrological opinion is to plant most flowers for an abundant display as the Moon passes through Cancer, Virgo or Pisces. Sow or plant out flowers noted for their beauty when the Moon is in Libra; for hardiness as she transits Taurus but for a reliable, sturdy plant one should wait until the Moon is in Scorpio.

Flowering annuals flourish best if planted out in the first or second quarter of Libra. Most biennials, perennials and bulb plants should be started during the decrease of the Moon.

PLANT	PHASE	SIGN
Aster	1 or 2	Virgo, Libra
Biennials	3 or 4	Cancer, Virgo, Libra, Pisces
Carnation	1 or 2	Cancer, Libra, Pisces
Chrysanthemum	1 or 2	Virgo
Carnation	1 or 2	Cancer, Libra, Pisces
Crocus	1 or 2	Virgo
Clematis	1	Libra
Daffodil	1 or 2	Virgo, Libra
Dahlia	1 or 2	Virgo, Libra
Flowering Dogwood	3	Cancer, Scorpio, Pisces
Gladiola	1 or 2	Virgo, Libra
Grass	1 or 2	Virgo, Taurus, Libra, Cancer
Honeysuckle	1 or 2	Virgo, Libra
Hop vine	1 or 2	Scorpio, Libra
Heathers	1 or 2	Libra, Scorpio
Hyacinth	3	Cancer, Scorpio, Pisces
Iris	1 or 2	Cancer, Virgo
Ivy	1 or 2	Virgo
Jasmine	1 or 2	Cancer, Scorpio, Pisces
Lily	1 or 2	Cancer, Scorpio, Pisces
Morning Glory	1 or 2	Cancer, Virgo, Scorpio, Pisces
Pansy	1 or 2	Cancer, Scorpio, Pisces
Peony	1 or 2	Virgo

PLANT	PHASE	SIGN
Petunia	1 or 2	Virgo, Libra
Pinks	1 or 2	Cancer, Virgo, Pisces
Poppy	1 or 2	Virgo
Rock garden	1 or 2	Libra, Scorpio
Rose	1 or 2	Cancer, Virgo
Sunflower	3 or 4	Libra
Sweet Pea	2	Cancer, Scorpio, Pisces
Tulip	1 or 2	Virgo, Libra
Vine plants	2 or 4	Virgo, Scorpio, Pisces
Wisteria	1 or 2	Cancer, Libra, Scorpio, Pisces

Strictly speaking, there are no such things as house plants, in the real sense. But, in general, whatever you do plant to keep indoors should be planted in the first or second quarter when the Moon is in Taurus, Cancer, Libra, Scorpio or Pisces,

If you do not like indoor plants you might like to consider having at least one pot of Aloe Vera available because of its remarkable healing properties in the event of burns, minor cuts or insect bites.

HERBS AND ASTROLOGY

Herbs have a wide variety of uses, and many, many moons ago they were the main source and general basis of society's medical pharmacopoeia. Today, herbs are now widely used by people in their cooking because they enhance an enormous variety of recipes, especially with the advent of so many different foreign cooking systems that have been introduced into this country in the past few years.

The best time for any herb is when it is reasonably young. All of these plants lose some of their efficacy as they grow older. Young plants tend to release their energies more easily than the older ones. It is one reason why the spring period is the better time for harvesting herbs in general although many may still have young shoots later in the year.

Despite the astrological advice given later, the best time to pick or dig up the herb of your choice is late in the evening, during the night or very early in the morning. Herbs that are gathered in for their flower use ought to be picked during the day time hours. Those you harvest for fruit or their seed are best taken during the night time hours.

Many herbs, like lavender for example, are used because of their delicate fragrance but, of course, quite a few herbs are still employed for their inherent medicinal values. Herbs tend to be grown for their flowers, leaves or seeds and most astrologers agree that, depending on which part of the plant you intend to use, the following guidelines should be observed.

If it is to use the flowers or the leaves, then plant in the first quarter under Cancer, Libra, Virgo or Pisces. To ensure a sturdy plant, Scorpio may be considered. For the best seeds, it is best to plant in the second quarter while the Moon is in Capricorn.

When picking or harvesting any herb, remember, that while the Moon is increasing to the Full, the plant retains a better and more fluid supply of its natural juices and essential oils.

With this in mind, always harvest herbs while the Moon is in one of the dry signs: Aries, Gemini, Leo, Sagittarius or Aquarius, preferably in the first or second quarter.

The following herbs are associated with the astrological signs as indicated:

Aries

Carnation, cayenne, cowslip, garlic, gentian, honeysuckle, hops, mustard, rosemary, chervil, basil, broom, nettles, catmint, wormwood, geranium and cypress pine

Taurus

Coltsfoot, lovage, mints, primrose, mint, thyme, goldenrod, violet, marshmallow, catnip, rose, carnation, saffron, jasmine, sage, tansy, wormwood, yarrow and soapwort

Gemini

Caraway, dill, lavender, parsley, vervain, mint, ferns, parsley, anise, marjoram, liquorice, fennel, honeysuckle, horehound, oregano and Lily-of-the-Valley

Cancer

Agrimony, balm, daisies, hyssop, jasmine, parsley, sage, aloe, evening primrose, myrtle, cinnamon, lemon balm, hyacinth, bay leaves, lettuce and water lily

Leo

Bay, borage, chamomile, marigold, mistletoe, poppy, rue, dill, lemon balm, tarragon, chamomile, clove, sandalwood, frankincense, camphor, eyebright and sunflower

Virgo

Fennel, savory, southernwood, valerian, chervil, dill, caraway, mint, morning glory, lily, horehound, lavender, endive and marjoram

Libra

Pennyroyal, primrose, violet, Yarrow, catnip, thyme, elderberry, iris, lilies, ivy, St John's wart, lemon balm and bergamot

Scorpio

Basil, tarragon, wormwood, catmint, basil, sage, catnip, honeysuckle, nettle, onion, coriander, garlic and elder

Sagittarius

Feverfew, houseleek, mallow, chervil, saffron, sage, basil, sage, borage, nutmeg and clove

Capricorn

Comfrey, sorrel, Solomon's seal, dill, tarragon, caraway, rosemary, chamomile, lamb's ears and marjoram

Aquarius

Elderberry, fumitory, mullein, daffodil, sage, comfrey, rosemary, valerian, fennel and mint

Pisces

Lungwort, meadowsweet, rosehip, sage, lemon balm, basil, lilac, nutmeg, borage, lilies and clove

Finally, it doesn't matter whether you are a layman or an astrologer, because there is one golden rule for all to observe. Never start or try to finish any task during a void-of-course moon period – very little ever comes of it, and whatever task you do start may have to be re-done later on.

Lunar Gardening Lore

THIS CHAPTER HAS been designed to help you to understand the general principles of gardening by, and through, the age and position of the Moon, using ancient and modern astrological lore. Please note the expression "general principles". None of this is set in tablets of stone because, just occasionally astrologers, like gardeners, will disagree with this "rule" or that piece of gardening lore.

In a few cases, some astrologers might tend to take into account the positions of the planets as well. But for our purposes, the positions of the planets, along with their mutual aspects, are not taken into account here, unless otherwise stated.

It is impossible to refer here to "normal" or everyday gardening procedures because of the lack of space. If, when the reader is referred to the wide variety of gardening manuals currently available, there will be a few anomalies that most people will take in their stride as a matter of course.

The general make-up of this lunar gardening guide is centuries old in parts, fairly new in others, and relatively modern elsewhere, because of so many and varied recent experiments that have been conducted by both gardeners and astrologers worldwide.

Over the past 50 years or more, I have collected and studied as much of the available material that I could. This data has been incorporated into each of the monthly recommendations that I wrote and that were formerly published by *PREDICTION magazine* for nearly fourteen years between 1990 and 2004, and again during 2011 and 2012.

THE AGE OF THE MOON

Each month the New Moon increases, grows or waxes in light to the Full Moon. It then wanes or decreases back to the next New Moon. Halfway between these two major points are the first quarter and the last quarter which are the mean positions or stages between the New and the Full Moons.

The secret of successful gardening is to know astrologically when to plant or sow different fruits and vegetables, flowers, bushes, shrubs, trees or herbs to maximise best results. Also, when there is no favourable time for such activities, there are hordes of other jobs and tasks both amateur and professional gardeners may involve themselves with. Such as, creating new fences and painting them, digging new ponds, attending to rock gardens, creating pathways, changing patches and beds for this or that, and so on, ad nauseam.

The First Quarter

As the Moon waxes from the New to when it is about Half Full, is the best time for gardeners to plant crops that produce their results outside of the plant, like asparagus, broccoli, Brussels sprouts, cabbage and cauliflower, or celery – there is a long list. Grain and cereal plants may be included here. There is always an exception to the rule; in this case, the cucumber, whose seeds are inside the fruit, but for some reason seems to flourish best if sown at this time.

The Second Quarter

Here, the Moon is increasing in light to the Full. Annuals that produce their yield above the ground do best when started now. Vines do well, as do the pulses, beans, peas, onions and peppers. Cereals and grains and tomatoes flourish especially in this period. If you are unable to work in your garden during the first quarter or perhaps are waiting for the Moon to transit a more suitable astrological sign, the second quarter can often be as equally productive.

The Third Quarter

This is when the Moon begins to wane to about halfway to its next new phase. Bulb and root plants yield excellent crops when started now. Biennials and perennials flourish beautifully as do most trees, bushes and shrubs. Quite a few berry plants, grapes, potatoes, onion sets and rhubarb do equally as well. Carrots, parsnips radishes and turnips yield excellent results when started during this period.

The Fourth Quarter

Sometimes called the Dark of the Moon because she is waning in strength and is now dying with little strength or influence until the next New Moon. This period is best given over to the more mundane garden exercises, so use the time to dig new patches, turn and cultivate the soil generally.

Weed, edge paths, clear lawns and guttering. Clean drains, destroy pests and get rid of rubbish by burning or taking it to the dump. Always keep the ash and remains of any bonfire – it helps promote growth when mulched in with other materials and it makes a splendid base for a compost heap.

GARDENING WITH THE MOON

Recognising these quarters, or phases, is just one part of the battle, for you have now to learn what to do as the Moon passes through each of the astrological signs – a very important point!

When you have learned how to coordinate the Moon's age, along with the sign she occupies at the times given in the ephemeris, you will begin to experience quite definite improvements in your garden.

The times given in the monthly listings are the moment the Moon enters each sign.

Unless otherwise stated, it is advisable to wait a little while to allow the full strength of that new influence to get under way. Allow at least half an hour to an hour for any place and time differential to take effect in most areas.

Moon in Aries

Because this is one of the Fire signs, logic determines this as a good period to have a bonfire to be rid of unwanted growths. Especially material that should be destroyed because it may be noxious or dangerous. Use the time to clean tools or electrical or mechanical machines. Also, cultivate, till and turn over soil.

Moon in Taurus

One of the Earth signs, so it is most productive. Almost anything may be planted or sown but in particular, beans, cabbage, garlic, onion sets, parsnips, potatoes, radishes and turnips. Flowers noted for their hardiness should be started now, for Taurus is a hardy sign. This sign also seems to favour fertiliser – apply as and when necessary.

Moon in Gemini

This is the first of the Air signs and it does not really favour planting or sowing. Destroy unwanted growths, weeds and pests. Turn soil and prepare areas for planting and sowing later. This is a dry sign and that makes it ideal for picking or generally harvesting crops especially in the last two quarters.

Moon in Cancer

The first of the Water signs, this is quite fruitful and ideal for watering, budding and grafting. You may also plant or sow out apple trees, asparagus, beetroot, Brussels sprouts, cabbage, carrots, cauliflower, endive, parsley, sage and spinach. Any flowers planted now will grow in abundance. Never cut wood when the Moon is in any of the Water signs.

Moon in Leo

Of all the signs, this is the most barren. Start nothing in this period at all. Once again, use the time for turning soil, cleaning up, repairing electrical or mechanical tools, or destroy pests and unwanted growths. It is safe to pick most vegetables and fruit now and lawns may be mown to help ease their growth.

Moon in Virgo

In this moist, but rather barren sign, quite a few gardeners plant their early spring flowers like crocuses, daffodils and snowdrops. Very often, flowers noted for their abundant growth do well when started now. Chemical killers for unwanted growths also seem to be more efficacious. It is not a good time for transplanting flowers, fruit or vegetables either.

Moon in Libra

This is perhaps one of the most useful periods for many activities. Flowers noted for their beauty and their fragrance flourish well and sunflowers always seem to grow with a sturdy stem. Plant beans, barley, beetroots and carrots – anything that has a root growth. Vines do well and seed for hay is most productive. Marrows, melons and peas should also yield excellent results when planted now.

Moon in Scorpio

Once again, this has proved to be a most productive sign, especially for bulb and gourd plants. Peppers, strawberries, tomatoes and all vine growths will produce extremely healthy results if properly looked after. Grafting and pruning exercises are best carried out while the Moon is in this sign, and it is the best time for creating a new compost heap.

Moon in Sagittarius

This barren and dry sign is often used mistakenly for harvesting fruit and vegetables but should not be. However, this is an excellent time for planting leeks, onion seeds and shallots. Leeks may always be left in the ground for longer than most, while shallots are known to multiply like crazy once you have started them.

Moon in Capricorn

This is not quite as fruitful as Taurus, despite being an Earth sign, but potatoes, radishes and even tomatoes seem to do extremely well if started now. The Moon passing through here will also help to encourage the handling and training of most animals. After grafting or if cutting back wood-stemmed plants, healing seems to be especially helped.

Moon in Aquarius

This last Air sign is very barren and extremely dry and should never be used for planting or starting anything.

This is a good time to catch up on cleaning debris and cleaning drains and guttering. Turn soil or prepare new areas for receiving new planting, but do not actually DO anything. However, harvesting and storing fruits are particularly recommended.

Moon in Pisces

As expected, this last Water sign is extremely helpful and especially encourages all root growth. One rule of thumb used by a many astro-gardeners is that, if they are unsure about when to start anything, this is the sign that will usually provide a good result. Start celery, plant chicory and rhubarb. If unsure about which flowers to prepare, please note that most started from seed in this period tend to flourish.

Those who want to include Flower, Leaf, Fruit and Root days in with this information are welcome to do so. However, if you find that this data seems to complicate issues, then ignore it and be guided by the information given in the relevant chapter for each month.

Void-of-Course Moon

FROM A PURELY astrological point of view, one should never start or try to finish anything when the Moon is in a void-of-course phase. For centuries, astrologers have advocated this, almost as a rule, rather than anything else.

As the Moon circles the Earth it takes her about 28 days or so and, during this time, she passes through her four major phases while she transits (passes through) each sign of the zodiac. The period between the last recognised, accepted or traditional aspect the Moon makes with another planet, and the time it enters the next zodiac sign, is called "void-of-course" by astrologers.

For centuries, it has been maintained that this is a time fraught with problems and, depending on the sign involved, almost anything is liable to happen. During this period the Moon has nothing to influence its course, no direction, no set path.

At such times, this may last for only a few minutes or it could be as much as a day or even slightly over. However long it is, or whenever it does occur, may be summed up as a short silly season that, although it may happen regularly, rarely lasts for long. The following is as simple an explanation of a void-of-course moon that I can give for the reader to understand without becoming swamped down in astrological technicalities.

When we arrange to meet or agree to contact someone for business or pleasure, we would probably agree on a time and place to our mutual satisfaction, by saying we will do so. This is something we assume and take for granted more or less every day. We rarely question an action so basic that we hardly ever notice.

However, when things go wrong we do remember, and often blame, just about everyone and everything except ourselves. Perhaps what we should have done is looked at the Moon to see what position and condition she was in when we first made the arrangement. In addition, and, perhaps much more to the point, we should also have checked where she would be when we agreed to our meeting.

You see, when the Moon is apparently not doing anything, we don't seem to be either. Human affairs seem to go a tad awry without valid cause and nothing really gets going properly again until the Moon enters the next sign when life takes on a more coherent shape again.

Without an ephemeris, that is, the tables of the positions of the Moon and planets, you will not be aware of this. But with them, you can take advantage of these periods and change your luck. These guidelines will help you to plan matters a little better. Almost every other day the Moon can be void-of-course for at least a few minutes, but on some occasions the period can last for up to a day or even slightly more, but rarely for more than about 28 hours or so.

As we are concerned with gardening here, these situations could affect or upset any work you might want to do or actually do in the garden. The reader is invited to experiment with what is written out here.

Thus, when the Moon is void of course in:

ARIES *or the First House*

You may feel physically out of sorts. You could be basically unable to understand or decipher simple instruction leaflets. Avoid interviews. Make trial runs if about to start regular new routines. Be careful with sharp tools or unfamiliar equipment. Try to avoid direct competition.

Check all personal identification documentation is correct and valid for the purpose intended. You may not like the face you have to show the world. You will probably think of what you should have said or done after the event. Don't worry too much; it is doubtful if anyone else noticed.

TAURUS *or the Second House*

Ensure you have sufficient money, chequebook or credit cards with you. Where possible, avoid entering into any long-term financial commitments like hire-purchase, leasing, hiring vehicles or tools or arranging bank loans. Personal comfort may be upset in such a way that it is not possible to reset the status quo easily. This rarely has anything to do with your actual finances, for most of us tend to have periods of fluctuating poverty. Quite often, people are known to buy extra food or other kinds of supplies that they may feel are in low availability at the time – just in case! Once the period is over, the materials are used up in the normal way of things.

GEMINI *or the Third House*

It is easy to get lost, even in familiar surroundings, directions become hard to follow and people seem unable to give guidance, to you, that is. Others interfere just when you least need it and routine, especially where concentration is required, is disturbed. The boss wants you, partners need your help. Those whom you rely on turn in shoddy workmanship. Brothers and sisters or local people and events may become a source of frustration. There might be problems understanding others, or other people have trouble following your drift. There may be minor private or public transport irritants – even the phone is likely to go on the blink.

CANCER *or the Fourth House*

Family relationships become upset, relatives prove uncooperative and there is a tendency to argue about private matters in public and embarrassing scenes can occur. Domestic routine falls apart. It is a poor time to begin a diet or start a no-smoking campaign. You may be unable to express your emotions properly; the wrong things are said at the wrong time. People cannot always finish what they start or, while performing one task, a half-finished one elsewhere springs back to mind. Little things go wrong at home; fuses or light bulbs blow and if you go out you might fret as to whether or not you left the oven or something else on.

LEO *or the Fifth House*

Not the best time to have fun in the wrong places. It is better not to join in with the boss, even if he is in a playful mood. Games go wrong and children have the knack of upsetting the grown-ups without really trying, serious matters can dissolve into silly situations that we all experience from time to time. Not the best of times to start anything new unless your hand is forced. Hearts and flowers situations turn you off and dates go awry. Married folk seem to rub each other up the wrong way; hobbies become boring and relaxation hard to achieve. As a last resort, the TV set goes on the blink.

VIRGO *or the Sixth House*

Details somehow just don't, or won't, marry up and have to be checked and re-checked. Nit-pickers have a field day; people cannot spell even the simplest of words. Computer programs crash, your appearance goes haywire at just the wrong moment and secrets tend to be aired inadvertently by indiscreet people who should know better. Not the best of times to try to repair anything either, for that will only make matters even worse. The daily routine fails at the first hurdle; pets take a liking to the furniture and road-works start up right outside the window. Repairmen turn up out of time and the clothes or dish washer packs up without notice.

LIBRA *or the Seventh House*

Avoid arbitration or peace – making roles; public functions fail to start on time or are cancelled at the last moment. People don't take things as seriously as they should. Practical jokers seem to come into their own but, whatever their intention, things fall flat or may even cause an accident. Even the press can get it wrong by being more lurid or sensational than necessary. People in general bother you and close personal relationships are liable to run into almighty differences over the slightest thing. Personal habits tend to seem more public than usual – throat clearing, coughs or other habits seem to become more pronounced and infuriating.

SCORPIO *or the Eighth House*

Joint financial problems occur. People conspire against others or among themselves. Foodstuffs may go off, even when stored in the fridge. Secret love affairs come to light, Scandals are revealed. Sexual tension is probable. What you buy may not fit the bill. Dustbins don't get emptied on time. Paper boys deliver wrongly or not at all.

Simple losses occur and the items are frequently never seen again. Some relationships might not be all that normal. Partner's habits may upset. Joint finances or tax returns could give cause for concern. Savings may not be up to the mark and the chances of investing but possibly losing money do not appeal at all.

SAGITTARIUS *or the Ninth House*

Impatient and restless and you tend to either over-reach yourself or you may over-overplay your hand. You feel you are in the right until shown you are quite clearly in the wrong. All travel matters, whether over short distances or long-haul air flights, somehow seem to conspire against you. You may go from A to B only to find your luggage has arrived at C. Anything (seemingly) straightforward develops snags and you become unable to think straight and solve the problem. In-laws can behave like the comedians claim, and it isn't funny. Students seem unable to study properly or duck classes at the wrong time for the wrong reasons.

CAPRICORN *or the Tenth House*

Anything to do with work and/or career matters can, and probably will, go wrong. Instructions are misunderstood or printed material is completely misinterpreted. Postpone precision work of any kind and defer all important decisions until a more propitious time. This is not the time to break or even bend the rules. If out and about and driving yourself, stay within the speed limit of the area. Don't trust your inner intuition, stay with the facts – if you can get them. Don't go down one road, only to change later. You may begin to wonder if you are in the right job and parents' side with the opposition. There is cause for considering a hermit's life.

AQUARIUS *or the Eleventh House*

Social relationships don't go the way you originally planned and there will be difficulty making decisions or getting others to make them. Urgent matters get bogged down for all sorts of reasons. Ideas abound, but little action is taken to implement them. At home or elsewhere, the central heating, gas or electric seems to take on a life of its own and computers especially will have a knack of doing exactly the opposite of what you want. People make promises but fail to honour them. You may consider re-directing your ambitions into another field of endeavour entirely but, after due consideration, you realise what you have is the best – for the time being, anyway.

PISCES *or the Twelfth House*

Domestic plumbing often goes wrong and the weather changes sufficiently enough to wreak havoc with any kind of outdoor activity – including drying your laundry. Indoors, the office system fails miserably. Files are not where they are supposed to be. Electrical equipment takes on a life of its own. In hospitals, the patients find restraint hard to contend with and an operating theatre takes on a new meaning altogether. Travel across water is not recommended. Surveyors find dry rot or the damp course is faulty. Should anyone tell you that you are not behaving logically, something seems to snap. You might laugh about all this later but only if the damage has been resolved satisfactorily.

General Weather Expectations

A SURVEY THAT ranged from around the turn of the previous century through to the 1950's, showed that, here in the UK, we seemed to suffer five seasons and not the expected four that comprise of spring, summer, autumn and winter which we have normally come to expect.

When the author of this survey broke his findings down in order to classify them properly (from his point of view, of course) he maintained that we have an early spring followed by spring, then an early summer, more or less together. This was followed by high summer and our often moderate and fairly sedate autumn, which then merged into what he called early winter, after which came late or proper winter.

As we have always said that we have only four seasons, much of what he discussed has just faded away. Most of our modern knowledge and weather lore has been handed down to us through the years, starting with what the ancient Egyptians allegedly first discovered, through their astrologer priests.

No matter to whom we assign any credit here in the UK, we enjoy a wide variety of conditions for such a small area. What we have done over the years is rely on what happened in more recent times. So that, for instance, we speak rather glowingly of the best summer we ever had, which was in 1976, or the worst winter, which many maintain began in late December 1962 and lasted through to around early March 1963.

Indeed, the weather we experienced in the latter part of 2011, the winter of 2012 and the excess rainfall throughout almost the whole of that year in the UK, has rather dented the averages to be expected in the next few years.

But this is dealing with the extremes rather than the averages, which are far more comfortable to experience. So, with this in mind, we will start with what we can generally expect from each month in far more moderate and average terms. As a rule, the UK is divided into two areas, north and south, and this will suffice for this survey.

January

Generally, this tends to be the coldest month of the year with temperatures that can range from below zero° centigrade to around 2° to 8° centigrade, it being a tad colder the more north one goes. There are often high winds in the more open spaces in the northerly areas, where we may experience at least 8 or 9 days of gales and storms. The south of the country barely suffers such rigorous weather, for the tendency here is to enjoy more sunshine. Rainfall ranges from about 7 or 10 centimetres in the south, to 25 centimetres or so in the north. There is almost always snow on the high ground.

February

No matter what sort of optimist you may be there is always a frost of some kind this month and temperatures range on average from about 4° to 9° centigrade. As a rule, it is a windier month in the north with a little more sunshine in the south of the country. The longer day is slowly beginning to be noticeable and rainfall is generally less this month – about 5 or 6 centimetres in the south with around double this amount the further north one travels. Snow persists but is much thicker in the north while the south often has none at all – but don't be fooled for it can be very heavy.

March

By now, the UK should be all experiencing much warmer weather, although there will still be frosts, and some of these can be quite severe. Daylight becomes obviously longer and the clocks go on at the end of the month. The rule is to advance the clock by one hour (spring forward) at 02.00 hours on the last Sunday night in the month. Cloud cover may last longer, although we all tend to see more actual sunlight this month. Rainfall ranges from around 5 centimetres to 25 centimetres or so, but low-lying areas become prone to flooding as snow on the high ground begins to melt.

April

Despite spring having arrived finally this month, one should still beware of sudden cold snaps and frosts, especially at night, which can be most severe. The winds tend to calm down into stiff breezes but the temperature change between night and day is very noticeable. Generally, they seem to range from between 4° through to 12° centigrade. Sunshine throughout the whole area tends to last for much longer periods. April showers do exist and they can be frequent, although they rarely seem to last for any real length of time. Snowfall is more or less over, although the extreme north can have the odd flurry or even stronger spells.

May

The nights can be fairly cold but the days are much warmer. There is still the danger of sudden frost. So, look after any or all fruit plants for, if they are in flower, just the one frost will undo all the good work. Quite often, this can be quite a windy period. Generally speaking, cloud cover is always apparent but may be restricted to the eastern side of the country. Rainfall eases back although there may still be a few very heavy moments. Temperatures can be as low as 7° to 9° centigrade overnight, while during the day, they can reach as high as 20° or 22°centigrade. Snowfall is rare.

June

Once June arrives, the summer isn't usually far behind. Fairly comfortable nights precede some fairly quiet warm days and it all becomes far more bearable as the month progresses. There is rarely a frost to worry about, for the temperature may range from 12° centigrade at night, through to around 24° centigrade during the daytime. On average, rainfall is rarely more than 10 to 12 centimetres anywhere. Wind can be a troublesome affair, especially on open ground or in built up areas between high sided constructions. It would be most unusual to experience frost or snow during June, but I have known snow on midsummer's day – 24 June.

July

If not the hottest month, it is certainly one of the warmest with temperatures reaching very high numbers – often as high as 27° centigrade or even more. Humidity can also be high, especially at night. This allows a gardener to slow down a little and pursue his or her tasks at a more leisurely pace. As a rule, there is a risk of thunderstorms in the final week, more frequent in the south rather than the north. Curiously, any winds we experience tend to be stronger in the north. Often, it becomes a shade cooler as the month draws to a close.

August

This is often a hot, sultry month with light rainfall everywhere, so you should be prepared to water the garden yourself. Temperatures can range from around 12° centigrade to very high numbers in all areas, certainly in the middle few days of the month. August is noted for its long steady spells of sunshine, with rainfall rarely more than 6 or 7 centimetres. However, in the closing two weeks or so, there may be sudden thunderstorms mostly over the high ground and more toward the north of the country. Snow is most unlikely except on very high ground in the far north – if at all.

September

While you may still enjoy a few more quite warm summer days, you will notice the way daylight time has begun to shorten, and it will be a tad chillier at night. The winds will pick up and there may even be gales in some places, Rainfall in all areas will become noticeably more frequent and will range from anywhere between 7 to 19 centimetres or more. Temperatures will remain summery for the most part, but the nights can fall to frost levels in some sheltered spots. Snow falls are rare this month but very high parts of the north might get a spattering.

October

As the temperature starts to fall, you will observe autumn arrive as all the summer colours deepen and change. Night frosts are more than likely to precede still fairly warm daytime hours. However, the winds tend to pick up and blow the leaves off trees, rather spoiling the marvellous colours of the period. Rainfall will increase everywhere and range from between 6 centimetres in the south to as high as 18 in the north. The clocks go back this month and the rule is to turn back the clock by one hour (fall back) at 02.00 hours on the last Sunday night in the month.

November

Winter is now upon us with frequent low cloud covering and temperatures that can drop quite dramatically in a few places, especially at night. Stormy weather, gales even, may be expected in most parts. Nevertheless, the autumn warmth still manages to show itself on a few of the better days, when we may expect anything from 2° to 12° centigrade depending on where you are. Rainfall also has a quite wide range from around 5 centimetres in the south to around 25 centimetres or so in the northern areas. In some places, the rain may give way to snow, although this is more likely in the northern areas.

December

Winter now begins to take a firmer grip in most places, although we can experience some fairly nice but rather weak sunny days everywhere. Winds can be bitingly cold and a few gales are likely. Frosts can be heavy and, with the ever-shorter days, many will yearn for the hazy, lazy days of summer. Temperatures usually range from below zero to about a measly 7° centigrade.

Snowfall rarely lasts for very long in the south and, while we can expect the possibility of a white Christmas, the usual post-Christmas bad weather is likely in the last week of the year, so wrap up warm if you go out.

The foregoing paragraphs are, quite literally, the averages as compiled from the UK weather experienced over the last one hundred years or so. They are quite accurate and, if or when you do heed them, you won't go far wrong when your pay attention to the needs of your garden through the year.

And, of course, at this stage all gardeners, irrespective of their skills, are well aware of what they ought to do as the year progresses.

Lunar Weather Lore

WHEN WE ADD astrological or lunar lore to gardening, a whole new world opens up. Experience has shown that, by adding the following information to what we already know in the purely practical sense, all aspects of what people do in their garden or on their farm takes on a completely new perspective. The success rate of what is grown can double in many cases.

Readers must not worry about any of the astrological data referred to here, for later in the book everything has been taken into consideration. You will not need to learn any new techniques in the astrological sense, for it has all been taken care of for you.

We now turn to what we may expect when each moon phase begins. But before we do that, we have to explain what we mean by the expression "moon phases"; how to find them, and why we say what to do at these times.

It has long been a tradition to refer to the Moon as "she" or "her" as, in astrology, she represents the feminine side of nature.

The Moon is the fastest of the heavenly bodies and (she) takes about a month to pass through the individual signs at a rate of about one sign every other day, on average. As a rule, she travels at slightly different speeds which vary from day to day, week to week and month to month.

The faster she moves the more perceptive people are likely to be and the more speedily things seem to get done. When she moves more slowly people generally tend to find it hard to understand anything new and tasks seem to be achieved more slowly.

The Moon is said to rule the instinctual side of our nature, our moods or unconscious responses to our daily life. Old habits die hard. She reflects an influence or power rather than actually starts anything new of her own because (in astrology) she is said to show no light (or powers) of her own. Thus, for many, the Moon is all things to all men…and women, of course.

LUNAR PHASES

At the New Moon, also called the First Quarter, she is conjunct, or in the same place as the Sun and is at the start of her waxing phase. On average, if there is going to be any rain it will be between now and the Full Moon. The sky tends to be somewhat clearer during daylight hours.

The First Quarter begins when she is in a square aspect with the Sun, or halfway toward the Full Moon when she will then be in opposition aspect to the Sun. Rain in this period tends to be heavy and can last for some time.

The Full Moon occurs when she is in opposition to the Sun. Here she is at her strongest point and, for the most part, her energies and powers at are their highest. At this halfway point in her cycle there is usually more chance of rainfall during the daytime hours than at night.

The Last Quarter begins her waning phase and as she begins to weaken, she is said to be disseminating her energy and strength. Any cloud and rain directly overhead is likely to pass fairly quickly and the sky remains reasonably clear.

At these major points of her cycle, the weather conditions indicated are usually experienced and, in addition, according to the time of the change, the following weather is possible.

A moon phase change of any kind between 24.00 and 02.00 hours during the summer months often indicates fair weather. When the change occurs during the winter one may expect frosty conditions.

Should the change occur between 02.00 and 04.00 hours during the summer, it will be cooler than usual and showers are likely. In the winter months this change suggests snow and possible stormy periods.

The change that occurs between 04.00 and 06.00 hours in both the summer, and the winter times often heralds rainy periods.

A change between 06.00 and 08.00 hours in the summer time presages a reasonable rainfall while during the winter months it implies heavy rain to mild stormy conditions.

A moon phase that begins between 08.00 and 10.00 hours suggests a period of changeable weather – neither one thing nor the other. In the winter, it can indicate a colder period with some rain or snow likely.

If the change starts between 10.00 and 12.00 hours, rainfall and/ or persistent showers are likely. In the winter time, the weather will become colder and there may be a fairly strong windy period.

An early afternoon moon phase change between 12.00 and 14.00 hours in the summer or the winter presages rainfall, with local conditions deciding how much.

If the phase occurs between 14.00 and 16.00 hours in the summer the weather will become changeable. In the winter time, the implication is for a milder period to take place.

A moon phase change between 16.00 and 18.00 hours in both the summer and the winter time, usually indicates fair weather for a few hours even if the skies are cloudy at the time.

Between 16.00 and 18.00 hours, a moon phase change in both the summer and the winter period suggests the weather will be variable.

Much the same occurs when the change happens between 18.00 and 22.00 hours in the summer, but in the winter, there may be a slight frost.

This series ends with a change in the phase of the moon between 22.00 and 24.00 hours. In the summer it suggests the current weather to continue as is. During the winter period, the weather tends to become slightly milder but at night there can be an extra bite to the frost.

THE PLANETS

In astrology proper, the procedures to adopt and follow are far more complex and involve setting up a chart, map or horoscope for the time and place, but this a book for a gardener and not an astrologer.

None of this has any real value here for we are more concerned with what we may tangibly note and use. However, having said that, it should be noted by amateur weather forecasters that each planet is associated with certain weather conditions.

Mercury, the swiftest planet of them all and also known as the Messenger of the Gods, has always been associated with the wind, its strength and direction. Often, it seems to be the cause of all manner of effects where winds of all kinds are concerned – from the faintest of breezes through to gales and storms.

Venus is the planet we tend to use when we look for possible rainfall and damp conditions generally. In cold weather she helps produce hail or snowstorms. She doesn't seem to have anything to do with temperature movement.

Mars, however, does have a lot of influence here and is usually held responsible for the upper temperatures we experience. Such ups and downs may be with or without rainfall, for it brings excessive dryness and even drought conditions. It can sometimes be responsible for stormy weather depending on the relationship it has with other planets in an astrological weather at the time.

Jupiter almost always brings fine and dry spells, but is rarely the cause of the kind of dry heat Mars may bring. At certain times, it can be held responsible for stormy weather but, in general, it favours the farmer and gardener well.

Saturn in a weather chart is most unhelpful as a rule. It lowers the temperature, brings cloud and rain and is responsible for the grey gloomy times. In the winter it brings cold wind, hail and snowfalls. When the air is still, it may herald foggy periods.

Uranus influences sudden changes of any kind, at anytime, anywhere. It will also lower temperatures and create wintry periods that can become quite stormy. When excessively aspected, it helps to produce severe gales, tornadoes and minor hurricane type weather.

Neptune as a planet on its own, has little influence and is regarded as a "still" planet. However, when aspected and, depending on where that aspect is from, it can be responsible for freak conditions. At all other times it seems to bring light rain. In cold weather it may start a sudden thaw.

Pluto (not strictly recognised as a planet anymore!) will either produce cool reasonably even spells or when badly aspected it will bring violent and extreme weather. Storms or hurricanes are possible, as are severe hot or cold periods. Once it has been activated, its influence can be rather severe.

THE SIGNS

Each of the Sun-signs is associated with weather conditions, although there ought to be a planet in the sign and, in simple terms for the layman, it needs to be activated by an aspect from another planet. Once again, an astrologer has to raise a map for the event, but this is beyond our remit for this book.

Nevertheless, depending on which planets are involved, for there may be more than two to assess and what the aspect (or aspects) may be, we can determine the weather for the area and time period involved.

Aries

This Cardinal Fire sign is very warm and rather dry and one that can sometimes be responsible for winds that can be very strong at times.

Taurus

This Fixed Earth sign is both cool and rather wet but, generally speaking, it tends to be the farmer's friend, for it has a moderating and steady influence.

Gemini

This Mutable Air sign is rather cold and dry. Under a strong influence, it keeps the clouds moving but temperatures may fluctuate.

Cancer

This Cardinal Water sign tends to be cool, rather wet and, if the right influences abound, downpours are likely – but they don't usually last very long.

Leo

This is a Fixed Fire and rather dry sign with a hot influence on weather. However, it maintains the same still influences for some time. In the winter it helps snow to melt.

Virgo

This Mutable Earth sign tends to be more of a cold and dry sign that creates high winds and can be the cause of blustery weather.

Libra

This is a Cardinal Air sign and is rather more of a cool sign than anything else, that helps to keep good weather overhead, but breezes can be strong at times.

Scorpio

This is a Fixed Water sign and, if we are to suffer extremes of weather, this will be the most responsible area to check. It intensifies whatever may be influencing us at the time.

Sagittarius

An Air Mutable sign, it tends to bring us dry, pleasant summery spells. Usually a warming influence and if strong in the winter period, it eases a cold spell and induces thaw conditions.

Capricorn

This is a Cardinal Earth sign and, if the aspects are right, expect severe weather in the winter, for this is a cold and oppressive sign. In summer months it brings excessive hot and or wet weather.

Aquarius

This Fixed Earth sign can make the weather quite changeable, that is, dry one minute, and damp the next. Warm or cold, it may bring thunder and lightning with stormy periods likely.

Pisces

This last Water sign is Mutable, whose overall nature is damp but cool and rather mild. We rarely have bad weather when this sign is strongly aspected.

Trees, Bushes and Shrubs

IN ORDER TO ensure that any tree in your garden, or on land that you own, does not lead into any kind of a dispute with anyone close – like a neighbour for example, you must see that you do not place one too close to any adjoining property.

Initially it might not have been that close, or one may have been put in before you took over the land, because people so often fail realise just how high a tree might reach. You need to consider the eventual height and spread that a tree is likely to attain. In time the overhang might restrict light or what they may want to plant – the roots of a tree really do multiply beyond belief in some cases.

There are legal positions and restrictions in both cases and they may also apply to other neighbouring trees that overhang the property you own.

If, for example, you want to cut back or remove branches that overhang your garden from your next-door neighbour, you must first enquire of them if they are prepared to cut them back first. Should they decline, and the tree is not protected by what is known as A "Tree Preservation Order" (TPO), then you may legally prune it – but be reasonable.

You may make any cutback on your side of your joint boundary be it a fence or a hedge, but you are not permitted to trespass on to his or her property and you are expected to offer what you do prune back to them first. If they don't want any of it then it, becomes your responsibility to clear it away properly – nothing may be left in their garden without their permission.

Should the tree have a TPO or is in a conservation area, you must approach the local authority for their permission before you do anything. You will find out this information from your local authority.

There is almost no legal protection in respect of any loss of light that may be caused by a deciduous tree or trees, and what there is, applies only to the windows of the actual property and not the garden. However, should the hedge be an overly high evergreen hedge then the local authority has certain powers to instruct a hedge owner to reduce the height or face a fine.

So, what exactly is a tree?

When it looks like a shrub because some of the growths have been trained to look like a small tree with a single stem or several stems that branch from ground level.

A pollarded tree is one that had its branches cut back close to the trunk or has been coppiced – cut from near ground level every few years to restrict the size and more or less given a new shape. A tree may be subjected to topiary – that is, cut into a small compact ornamental shape or a wall shrub, as if it were a small tree grown flat against a sheltered wall.

The reader may now gather that a "tree" may be, therefore, a growth as against a plant in the most simple of terms. It may grow and grow and grow, or it may remain at a reasonable height, year in and year out, depending upon what it is and how it is looked after.

HOW TO LOOK AFTER TREES

First of all, what type of tree are you about to put in and, more importantly – where?

You should place a tree where you know it will grow quite happily for many years. Should you want to move house a few years later, you may not be able to get at it. Thus, if you do have some idea, it would be best if you plant it in a large pot (2–6 or 10 litres, depending on the tree) where it will grow for around ten years or so, and then you can take it with you when you do go. Use the topsoil from the garden, mixed up with a small amount of peat free compost, some time before you do move off.

Should you want to place trees out somewhere in the grounds think well before you put anything anywhere. Whatever else you may do, don't just plant trees willy-nilly close to the house or your walls, because the roots will eventually interfere with the house foundations sometime later on. Different tree types prefer different conditions. Some might need to be in full sun, full shade or partial shade or in soils that are loamy, chalky or clay based.

It is really important that you take away all the wrapping around the tree as soon as you can and then add a small amount of water into the plastic bag that has almost certainly been placed around the root system. Try to keep your new tree root moist and away from direct sunlight until you are ready to plant it which should be as soon as you can. It won't hurt to hold it in a pot until such time.

Generally speaking, you should plant all trees, irrespective of their particular type, sometime between October and April – late winter to mid–spring, to get the best results. Trees are wonderful additions to any garden and they can live hundreds of years, with the right help.

Should you plant in the spring, you will need to take very special care because the tree may have begun to bud early – to grow and form fresh leaves. While deciduous trees come back each year, your tree may not be of this type and must be planted quickly in a prepared place and then thoroughly watered. In sunny spring weather, a deciduous tree can often bud much earlier than expected.

Yet again, the summer is not a good time to plant out any tree, for they really do need all their natural energies to grow during this period. It might be better to place it in to a pot and water the root area as soon as you can and then on a daily basis thereafter. Don't water the leaves, for they will attract the sun and this might make them act like a magnifying glass, in which case the sun could easily burn small holes through them.

During the autumn period, deciduous trees lose their leaves and then become dormant until the following spring. This is quite natural and now, or a little later into the season is a good time to plant a tree, for this gives it plenty of time to settle in prior to the winter period.

Ideally, winter is about the best time to plant trees because most of the many varieties sleep, and that means that placing your new tree in a new home will not upset any natural balance. However, don't plant a tree during icy weather but do ensure that you protect the roots from frost until you can.

Citrus Trees

Of course, there are always a few variations on a theme when it comes to tress. For example, a citrus tree is an outside plant that will need a lot of help to become protected against frost. These plants give year-round pleasure with their fragrant flowering buds gradually growing into their fruiting period.

Now, during the spring, and as the weather gradually becomes warmer, sunnier and brighter, you need to take extra special care because sun-room temperatures or conservatories and greenhouses can soar.

As the frost decreases and summer begins to wear on, temperatures will rise. Now is a good time to move the tree outside – end of May beginning of June is a good time but it will depend on our (English) weather. It is best to site the tree in a shady spot at this time. After a week or so, it can be moved into full sun position for the rest of the summer. Citrus trees love sunny weather, so the more the merrier. However, should you want one indoors, then make sure it is near a window in a cool room.

As and when the autumn period begins to settle in, you may move any outside plant back indoors, preferably before it begins to get too chilly or windy usually around the end of October and the beginning of November.

Before the winter period really takes hold, either bring citrus trees indoors or keep them in a reasonably heated greenhouse. They need plenty of light and will do well if near, or by, a south facing window. Try to maintain a continuous temperature somewhere between 4° – 15°C. Any sudden changes are quite unhelpful to these rather sensitive plants.

Don't put any of these trees in water for any reason. If it appears to have dried up, then gently water the compost, which may well be every day in sunny summer weather, and about every two or three weeks in the winter. Keep the watering can in the same room so that the temperature will be kept even. Also, it doesn't hurt to add citrus feed to these watering times. As a rule, these trees tend to keep their shape so that pruning, if any, may be kept to an absolute minimum. A snip here and there should be all that is needed at any time.

Fruit Trees

Fruit trees are quite different and their roots must be kept dry and away from sudden temperature changes in any season. Pruning is best carried out by removing unnecessary branch growth, leaves or stem extensions during the winter period. These essentially garden trees almost always need protection against frost. Once spring has arrived, they really will flourish in any sunny position preferably close to a fence, hedge or wall to help protect against wind or surprise frosts. They usually blossom in the spring and will probably be pollinated by birds or the local bee population unless it is self-pollinating, like an apple or pear tree.

In the summer, these plants positively adore the Sun and need a lot to help ripen their fruit. So, keep your fruit tree in a sheltered position that receives a lot of sunshine to get the best result. Some trees will need protection from garden birds, or they will take the small fruit as the blossom falls away. Simple small squared netting usually does the trick quite well.

During the autumn is the best time for most fruit trees, because of their offering. As fruit ripens, and is picked or drops away to the ground, gather it all in and store in a cool but airy place. As a rule, you should try to water fruit trees daily during sunny summer weather. It will also be helpful to them if you could find the time to ensure they are well fed. Nutrients for their energy, to grow and remain healthy, should be given at least once a month during the summer, preferably with an organic fertilizer.

They don't need pruning that often but their branches will almost always be looking for more space. In which case a simple snip from the ends of these little growths should be enough to encourage new branches further back and create a nice bushy tree in good general condition. Pruning is best carried out mid-winter in December or January.

ORNAMENTAL TREES AND BUSHES

As long as you remember to water the soil more or less each day during hot and dry periods and keep the roots well drained, they will seem to go on forever. Also, these plants live out in the open all the time and will need protection against frost.

In the spring, as the weather becomes sunny and brighter, it is important to make sure that these types of plants are allowed to stay in sunny positions nearby to a fence, hedge or wall to help protect from the wind and frost.

As the summer gradually disposes of the danger of a frost, it is permissible to move them to a good position, until the summer gives way and the more autumnal weather begins to work its way in. Then, if need be, by all means move them again to where you consider the best place might be in your particular garden. Try not to over water because this can be quite more harmful. Once a day will suffice in hot summery weather, but once or twice a week should be enough otherwise.

Keep a good weather eye open for the first frost of autumn or until the weather really begins to have a chill in it, and put them back up against the protection of the fence, hedge or wall, which will probably be around the end of October. It won't hurt to keep your ornamental trees in the same full sun position south facing during the winter period. These plants are evergreens and must have a lot of light during winter, especially if there are strong winds with which they may have to contend.

To keep these plants looking good all year-round, it won't hurt to re-pot them after about six months or so of getting them. Their roots need to be kept clean and free from possible infection and this exercise will ensure they do remain healthy. As you re-install them you can check what is needed quite easily. Pots should have good open holes for drainage and a layer of stones at their base will help. Fill with fresh clean top soil.

Should any of these plants need pruning, snip with a good pair of secateurs when branches or leaves start to get out of hand. Pruning should be little and often and is better done in the spring and early summer months – but only if needed.

Roses

It is imperative that any new rose you buy or are given is removed from its wrapping as soon as possible. Work in some water – not too much – to its new container or hole in the ground, and plant the bush reasonably quickly. Add a little water each morning to the root area in dry weather. As this is a deciduous plant, you won't get to see too much until early spring, when buds start to appear. In good sunny weather, this may happen earlier than you expect.

Much care will be needed if planting out in the summer. The roots (never the leaves) must be watered regularly. Also, remember to "dead-head" (take away dead, dying or superfluous flower heads), for this encourages growth. While you are at it, be on the look-out for the variety of summer pests and treat them according to which type they are.

As autumn closes in, these plants will start to lose their leaves and, as they go, so do the flowers die off, leaving a pretty awful looking plain remainder. This is just about the best time to plant fresh roses and also to carry out pruning exercises. The book says this ought to be carried out during September and October, but a little later won't hurt.

The stems and/or unwanted braches should be cut back to any point you wish, but if there are any buds showing, or if there is a fork in the wood, trim to just in front of this. Clear away the debris, which will help to avoid the possibility of disease. Leave until late spring or early summer, when you ought to re-appraise how things are going then.

Planting Trees

Most fruit trees should be planted when the Moon is in Taurus or Libra, although the apple should be planted when the Moon is in Sagittarius. You can see from the list below that quince trees should be put in during the first or second quarter, when the Moon is in Capricorn.

From an astrological point of view, we tend to look at trees in general as "perennials" and much prefer to use the third quarter Moon for planting. This is probably more for astrological technical reasons, than actual gardening ones. When a plant is put in during a decreasing Moon, it helps create a better root formation and the slower growth of the top of the tree becomes better protected. Trees in general, that are planted during this period will often have a slightly thicker bark and almost always have a longer life.

Christmas Trees

To ensure your indoor tree remains in good condition and does not readily drop its needles a fir Christmas tree should be cut down just prior to the 11th Full Moon of the (calendar) year, which is usually in November (in 2016 this is in Taurus, on the 14th) but, just occasionally, it may occur in December. Spruce trees do, however, tend to lose their needles earlier than the fir.

Pruning trees

For the best results, one should prune a tree only when the Moon is waning and passing through Aries, Leo or Sagittarius. Equally, but with not quite such good results you may also carry out this exercise when the Moon is on the wane either in Gemini or Sagittarius.

Planting Trees

The best planting times for the various bushes, shrubs and trees will be found in the following list.

PLANT	PHASE	SIGN
Annuals	1 or 2	Libra
Apple tree	3	Taurus, Cancer, Sagittarius, Pisces
Apricot tree	2 or 3	Taurus, Libra, Capricorn
Ash tree	2 or 3	Venus, Jupiter
Beech tree	2 or 3	Capricorn
Cherry tree	2 or 3	Taurus, Libra, Capricorn
Deciduous trees	2 or 3	Cancer, Virgo, Libra, Scorpio, Pisces
Evergreen trees	2 or 3	Cancer, Virgo, Libra, Scorpio, Pisces
Fig tree	2 or 3	Taurus, Libra
Horse Chestnut	2 or 3	Taurus
Maple tree	2 or 3	Taurus, Cancer, Virgo, Pisces
Nectarine tree	2 or 3	Taurus, Virgo, Libra
Nut tree	2 or 3	Cancer, Scorpio, Pisces
Oak tree	3	Sagittarius
Peach tree	2 or 3	Taurus, Virgo, Libra
Pear tree	2 or 3	Taurus, Virgo, Libra
Plum tree	2 or 3	Taurus, Virgo, Libra
Quince	1 or 2	Capricorn
Trees (shade)	3	Taurus, Capricorn
Trees (ornamental)	2	Taurus, Libra

Ponds

THE ONE VERY serious consideration to be taken into account, is probably the one most people tend to forget. The majority of houses have their water supply metered, which means that every litre has to be paid for, whether you like it or not. The cost of running a pond can (initially) be quite considerable, depending on what you want to create.

You must now think of how to capitalise as best as possible, not only on how to conserve your water supply, but also how to add to what you need in the cheapest way possible. It is a wise man who ensures that every drop of water that falls into the garden is preserved in some way.

So, by planning well ahead and thinking through what will be needed, as against what you hope you might get, you should be able to make sure you will have a plentiful supply the whole year round, and every year. You will need to invest in several water butts and place them where they will do the most good.

WATER BUTTS

When drought conditions are likely, there are several methods to conserve what does fall from the sky. This is one excellent way of preserving all water that comes into the garden. Conserving pure rain water in a water butt connected to the downpipe from your gutter is helpful in that, tap water isn't too well-liked by a lot of different plant life. In fact, many seem to flourish better when they take in rain water as an alternative. Water butts are ruled by the Moon, preferably when she is in Cancer, but Scorpio and Pisces may also be considered.

Down pipes around the house are placed so that they run into drains. Ensure that you place your new butts safely, so that they do not block any drains and you can still get to clean them as easily as before. Clean the guttering and remove all the unwanted debris, especially loose leaves and dislodged moss, before you connect anything. Do NOT divert waste water from the toilet system.

The butt has to be raised up, of course, to allow you to fill your watering can from the tap supplied. Wrap an old stocking around the bottom end of the down pipe for this will stop even more unwanted debris from going into the water. The saving here, when there is a lot of rain about, really is most satisfying.

WATERING

Try not to water your garden too late in the evenings. You see, when you do use your hose, you also water the leaves of your plants and if they cannot dry out overnight, they may start to decay. Rotting leaves can cause a plant to die, so water gently instead in the early hours, especially the roots of new or young plants.

You should also try to avoid watering around the midday period as well, because water tends to evaporate and the leaves will become scorched. Another useful tip is to throw away your sprinkler, because it really is most wasteful.

Water when the Moon is in the water signs of Cancer, Scorpio or Pisces.

However, I digress. So, back to the type of pond wanted. Is it to be a small one more for decorative purposes? A large one in which fish will be kept, or is it wanted just to attract wildlife? Ponds stocked with goldfish or koi carp do not attract wildlife so much, for such species are rarely compatible.

POND POSITION

Will the pond be surrounded by trees or be in shade? Dropping leaves can be troublesome, especially in the autumn, and very few pond plants grow well unless there is sufficient light. Does the garden have a slope to it? A cascade can, and does, look attractive but some waterfalls that have been built up on a flat area can often look hopelessly out of place.

Will what you want be seen more or less from every angle of the garden and house and will the type of pond want a liner or will you put in a pre-formed version? What size is wanted, what type of plant life were you considering, because different plants need differing water depth?

Most important of all is, will what is wanted require professional advice, or will you be able to manage on your own? And, after all these considerations, when are you going to put one in?

Ponds in general are ruled by the Moon and or Pisces and to begin work, right at the beginning, one should ensure the Moon is passing through Cancer, Scorpio or Pisces. Remember to double check the position you have chosen. Too much sunlight is unhelpful and may cause an influx of algae. Use a proper spirit level to ensure the finished article won't have what seems like an irregular surface to it.

For best results, use a dark coloured, good quality material for lining, because this does not reflect light so easily. Which also means you won't have to do it all again after five or six years. Initially, you will have to fill with it with tap water, but this is not always so good when it comes to refilling it.

ELECTRICS

You should make arrangements to place any pump and/or filters where you can always get at them easily. If, or when, they either go wrong or need to be cleaned and/or serviced, you need to be able to get at them readily. Any life in the pond can, and will, suffer if the pump or filter is out of action for too long, because you cannot get at them quickly enough.

Apart from noting all that you have to do and when to do it, decide if you are going to have a pump operated system to circulate the water. You must have an ultraviolet light to kill off the bugs and stop the water from turning green during the summer. You may well need to change this bulb every spring to ensure that it remains potent.

Should you want to fit a pump to circulate water and keep a fountain or a waterfall on the move, or even have a few outdoor lights to illuminate the area, you are going to need an effective power supply from nearby. This must be from a permanent supply, run underground from the house using toughened and waterproofed cable and not some other small piece of flex plugged in somewhere else. This kind of electrical work must be installed by a competent electrician, who will see that it conforms to all the necessary rules and regulations.

CREATING THE POND

Whatever size pond you are going to install, you are going to have to dig out some sort of hole first and you will need to place the surprising quantity of soil you create somewhere else. On top of that, you must time this for best possible results. It would be better to start this sort of task in the autumn, although it is not absolutely necessary. All holes are ruled by Saturn, so it won't hurt to start digging when the Moon is in Capricorn.

A hole this size, made just before winter sets in makes the open area far more receptive to the winter rains and frosts. You should create the hole to the depth you want for either a pre-cast shape, that you should be able to obtain from most garden nurseries or one for the alternative size and shape you have in mind. Carefully define the perimeter of the pond with string and when you start digging into the turf, stack it neatly away somewhere else for possible later use.

Start to dig to the level of where you want the first shelf to be and mark this out with string or chalk or a small stone or whatever else you think would be best to use. On this shelf, which will be covered by the water, you will put the pump. If you are going to have one together with the UV lighting, make sure this is always easily accessible from the side of the pond or any bridge you may build.

Now dig out the rest of the centre of the pond shape adding any other shelving levels, and continue until you have reached the depth you want. Use a spirit level to ensure each shelf is level. Next, check the sides of the pond, following the top shape you have envisaged.

This is now a good time to think things through again, and remember to make sure at least one side of the pond has a gentle slope to the water surface, so that animals like the hedgehog have a reasonable way of getting out if it should they fall in.

Make sure you get rid of any lumps, bumps, humps and/or sharp-edged material from the hole. It would be a good idea to now spread a small layer of builder's sand all over the area and especially at the bottom. This will help protect any liner from holes. It will not hurt to install a soft pond underlay or some old carpet above the sand to furnish extra protection from damage.

Ideally, you should now have someone with you to help lay in and position the lining material you have chosen. Spread it as evenly over the (pond) hole as you can. Try not to drag it over the ground. Set bricks or small stakes on top of, or through the extreme outer edge, and begin to fill the pond with water.

Every so often, stop the water flow and pull hard on the edges of the liner so that it fits neatly and as tidily as possible over all the bends, shelves and contours of the pond. Keep going along these lines until the pond is full.

Trim the liner, leaving about a 30cm (12in) overlap all around the side of the new pond. Cover this overflow with slabs of paving and then begin to create a more natural effect around the edge. It will take time, but in the end your new pond will soon lose the new look and begin to look as though it should belong there.

PROTECTION

While you are waiting for all this to happen, purchase some black small-hole netting of about 1cm or a ¼ inch, and also buy some tent pegs. Spread the netting fairly tightly over the water top at about 12cm or 5 inches high and hook it into the top of the tent pegs. This will keep any visiting heron out, but allow small animals in, and let birds feel safe when they come to drink or even bathe.

Also, during the autumn months you will be so pleased at how many leaves and other debris the netting will prevent from falling into the water. All you have to do is to keep the netting clear as much as possible.

Once wild birds are aware of the pond, try make sure you encourage the crows, rooks and/or magpies, because they simply can't stand herons at any price. Just watching them gang together and chase the larger bird away is well worth the effort.

GENERAL MAINTENANCE

Most ponds may be left for almost any length of time, for they tend to look after themselves without too much help from man. Should you put any plants actually into the water, make sure that at least one of them is a good oxygenator, otherwise position whatever plant life you like in and around the water.

Before you add any fish or other pond life, you should wait for a couple of months or so. If you want to add fish wait at least six weeks or so, until the plant life has become established.

You would be wise to have a chat with either a local pond keeper or visit the local nursery, where there will always be someone to advise you as to what type of fish and how many you should keep. He (or she) will advise you of temperature requirements, water depth and which fish lives reasonably peacefully with what other fish. They should also tell how many you ought to keep, according to the size, depth and type of pond you have created, and they will also advise on feeding.

Never just pour the fish into the water from what you have brought them home in. Lay the bag on the water surface for about an hour or so to allow the pond and pack temperature to become reasonably similar. Then undo the bag and just let the fish glide in.

How or where you install a waterfall or other feature will be dependent on how large the pond is and where you have placed it. You will have probably put your pond next to a hedge or bush and that is where you should site such a feature, for you can hide extraneous water pipes and cabling more easily.

Once the pond has water in it and you have laid a few plants around the edges, you will notice more and more animal life – especially the robin. Gradually, all kinds of pond life will start to appear. As if by magic, a toad or a frog will turn up, a snail or two or even a newt may arrive out of the blue. There are very few dragonflies that do not love ponds and the same goes for all their relatives as well.

Spring

Spawning time for most creatures occurs during the spring. At this time, there may be an absolute glut of eggs of all kinds laid as a matter of course, which all helps a pond to develop and grow the way you first thought. There will nearly always be someone somewhere who will help you reduce what you do get, but if you are forced to get rid of any excess, never put any down a drain or into a public stream or river, because you might be spreading disease. You may also have to clean your pumps and filters a little more than usual at this time.

Winter

During the winter period there is always a danger of frost when the pond may ice over. This won't hurt the fish much but other animal life will need to be able to get to normal air levels. Never break the ice with anything. The vibration could kill the fish. In the event that ice should occur, lay a small bowl on the water surface the night before. If it does get that cold, all you have to do is pour in some hot water and then just lift the bowl out.

The resultant hole left should be sufficient, while you work on making a bigger hole. Again, don't break the ice. Pour some more hot water into the bowl and let nature take its course. A log or small piece of wood laid from the edge into pond is another way of clearing ice from a pond surface. In the event of ice, all you need to do is simply lift the wood and a hole will appear. Some say a tennis ball or other size ball may be used, but they can freeze up too tightly to be removed that easily, but it is still an idea to bear in mind.

SAFETY

Finally, make sure no child, toddler or elderly person can fall in when visiting this brand-new feature in your garden. Keep access paths clean and clear at all times.

Garden Wildlife

AS A RESULT of the terrible weather conditions of late throughout the UK, Europe and elsewhere on the planet local and world, wildlife has in many places become virtually non-existent. In some areas this is a massive problem, a tad rare in others, but definitely too rare in many a domestic UK garden.

Whether we like it or not, we need these creatures because, in one way or another, they all help to make plants proliferate, grow to maturity, die, and (in some cases) come back again the following season. Until you actually see this enormous list of your known (and just as many unknown) garden allies that may inhabit just about all gardens, most people would be surprised, although staggered might be a better term.

In many cases, we spend a lot of time making sure some of these creatures are killed off, but today so many are just are not there in the first place. This can lead to poor results in your garden, no matter how hard you may try to make some of your plant life grow.

As a rule, the course of natural life, featuring the many varieties of the natural inhabitants of our gardens, tends to be a swings and roundabouts affair. Many of these little creatures just seem to disappear, only to re-appear at some time in the future. Now, it doesn't hurt to make little places for this small animal life to grow and mature, but within reason of course. Certain types of plants attract certain types of insects and other life which, in turn, encourages bird and other animal life behind, them for that is nature's way.

Some of this life is almost never welcome – moles, slugs and snails and those hideous outsize spiders that often like to visit us indoors, especially when we least expect them. But, despite your disdain, they too have their part to play in keeping your garden world balanced.

Many people, the ladies especially, positively hate these eight-legged invaders, so make a note of this simple remedy to keep them away, for it works every time. The ordinary common or garden horse-chestnut fruit, the good old-fashioned "conker" will do this trick and it always works. Simply place one or two on the floor by your back door(s), on the side window sills and the front door(s). Just leave them there until the next horse-chestnut crop is due, and then exchange the old for the new.

It DOES work. We haven't had a garden spider in our house for many years, ever since we started this habit. Spiders have an intense dislike of the smell these small nuts seem to have and they avoid them like the plague, all the time they are there.

Quite a few people have windows which open on to growths against the house or who have plant life that climbs up the outside walls. Feel free to open your doors and windows, as long as you leave a conker or two on the window sill to offset spiders who might want to use this method of house entry.

Pestilent insects in general, tend to have their own natural predator as a matter of course and these killers usually manage to keep control of the problem, as a rule, so that when you allow for the one, you must remember to allow for the other.

Creatures like ladybirds and lacewings seem to manage to keep aphid life well under control, and will be able to do so as long as you allow them in the garden. To keep this life-form happy, plant out some sage, rosemary, santolina and lavender in your herb garden to help them thrive.

Just these small creatures alone would normally be enough to bring some of the bird life into your garden, but to attract even more feathered friends, you should ensure you have a few bird boxes dotted about here and there. The nature of the location and the type of box will attract certain types of birds. Robins and wrens love open fronted boxes placed fairly low down but well hidden in the greenery.

Bats of all kind seem to have disappeared from most areas and new roosts are desperately needed to bring them back again. Of course, bats prefer to make their home in old mines, used or dis-used rail tunnels, caves, buildings and even old woodpecker holes, but they will live in boxes with a slit at the bottom in a robin-style creation. Bats feed a lot on insect life, which is another useful aide to keeping the quantity of the more troublesome mini-life down.

If you make sure you have plenty of leafy boughs all around the garden, you will attract all kinds of other birds. All members of the crow family, even jays, the different woodpeckers, wood pigeons, finches and chaffinches will all eventually come to recognise your garden, not only as a safe haven from their predators but also as somewhere they may eat.

While preparing to do any of this, please remember to establish which are the seed-eaters, and which are the nut-eaters, and arrange for it accordingly. Seed feeders are small round tubular containers with holes usually at the base from which birds gain access. These will attract creatures like the finches, tits and sparrows. The hopper type of feeder attracts the smaller birds like goldfinches and siskins. When these are placed on poles, make sure you grease the poles well, for that will ensure any squirrels can't shin up to help themselves.

Trays or the similar small surface feeders are better suited for the birds that prefer a more general cereal-based mix. These little bird tables are well liked by almost all the feathered life and please also remember to put out fresh water supplies.

What isn't drunk will provide a bath for the cleaner types. All food and water containers should be kept clean and well-filled as often and as much as you can. Sooner or later, you will find some of these sites are more visited than others. A quick survey may show you why, and you can adjust these places as and when.

For what it is worth, we are visited over the months by no less than 42 different kinds of our feathered friends, who come to feed and even bring their young to learn how to hunt, because we have created a home from home for them all.

But this isn't all about birds. If you keep your eyes open, you may spot a hedgehog snuffling along the base of any dense hedge or even a small pile of rubbish. They love tinned cat or dog food, or even a few old cooked vegetables you may have left over. They also have a liking for old (or fresh) cake and/or a biscuit or two is usually well received. It is NOT a good idea to feed them bread and/or milk, because it does them more harm than good.

They will make a home at the bottom of dense hedges and will even live in a small open box you might like to provide. They also feed on beetles, caterpillars, slugs, snails and worms. They hibernate during the winter period, so the box or nest will be (or if you do it, should be) lined with moss, leaves and all kinds of other garden debris.

Bees and wasps thrive in the right type of garden. If you plant the right flowers, they will descend in their droves to gather the pollen. Please remember that, if one of these creatures should land on you, it is not to hurt you. Please keep still and, after a few seconds, they will fly away. If, however, you should take a swing at them and miss, they will sting as a matter of self-defence.

Bees flourish best in hedges, trees and shrubs of all kinds. They adore broom, rosemary, roses, honeysuckle and buddleia. They also like a lot of other plants, especially all kinds of salvia, so you are advised to check locally for what seems to be the best for them in your area. We have a nest of honey bees living under the lining of one of our ponds so if we work on it at any time, we always make sure they can get in and out as freely as possible afterwards.

Wasps positively adore jam and cakes, if you leave them out. They tend to eat smaller insects and love caterpillars. Wasps also have a nasty habit of eating or laying their eggs in many different types of fruit. Birds tend to feed on both bees and wasps.

The grey squirrel inhabits many a garden or will visit because of the goodies they can steal. They eat (or will bury until later) acorns, other nuts and bulbs. They take buds, fungi of almost all kinds, and roots. They also steal quite shamefully from bird tables, especially if you have put out peanuts for your flying visitors.

Squirrels often carry off what they cannot eat, which is why you should always try to make sure they cannot get at what you do leave out for other life. Greasing the poles is one idea. Not siting the feeders too near a tree is another, although these creatures can jump enormous distances if they really must.

The butterfly and moth family also inhabit people's gardens. The wide variety of these creatures will dwell in our gardens for most of the year from mid-spring through to late autumn. While reasonably rare of late, we have observed many of these pretty little characters flying about this year.

The fox is usually a night visitor and, while it is fairly rare for them to create any real damage, they do have a habit of digging up small patches in lawn areas or, if you have buried a dead animal of any kind, they will sniff it out, dig it up and eat most of it, leaving you to clear up the mess they will leave behind. If there is a hole at the base of your perimeter fence, don't fill it in because that is the way foxes move around and through most gardens.

Badgers also visit at night foraging here, there and everywhere for what they like the most – berries, seeds, worms, frogs, rats and or mice and even a small lizard or two, if you have a pond. Moles we have dealt with elsewhere (see the chapter on *"Tips & Wrinkles"*).

A lot of people have garden ponds, and these can be quite a magnet for yet another wide variety of garden visitors during the day or at night. No life can exist without water, so don't be surprised at what you might find near or actually in your pond, no matter what size it may be.

However, a small but most essential point is to ensure you have at least one, possibly a couple of gently sloping areas from the garden level to the actual water level itself. This enables creatures like hedgehogs and other small mammals to get to the water, drink and leave safely afterwards.

You may not realise it at first, but your pond will almost certainly stock itself with all manner of life. Expect to find frogs, newts and even a dragonfly or two, with the odd damselfly who will breed here. Try to put a couple of small bushes near the pond, for this allows a bird or other animal to hide until it feels safe to come out. An old log placed in the pond helps birds to land away from possible predators and allows them to drink and bathe as they may see fit.

During severe winter weather, put a fair size ball into the water so that if it should freeze over you can easily remove it to allow creatures to visit and get to the water, and also to enable any pond dwellers to be able to get out. Never break the ice – the damage you could cause can be irreparable to whatever may live in the water underneath.

Most of us will have a small "dump" somewhere, usually at the very end of the garden – out of sight and out of mind. Nearby will be a small compost heap or a bin to keep it in. This will attract all manner of creepy-crawly insect life of a really wide variety of descriptions. Except for keeping it fairly tidy, it would be wrong to clear any of it away except, of course, for when you want the compost.

The whole point of this chapter is to allow you to appreciate the enormous amount of different wildlife of an equally wide variety of sizes and habits that could be found in your garden. None of us have all of them, but while we struggle to keep things as near normal as we can, it would be wise to familiarise yourself with as many as possible – just in case.

If you can spare the time, sit down somewhere nearby and watch for a while. You will see an incredible amount of small wildlife all of which, one way or another, will be useful to your garden. Even a small ant hill has its uses, for these inhabitants rarely create any real damage to your various growths. Their main diet relies on sugary matter, oily types of seed or the honeydew left on aphid-infected plants. Small insects like the aphid may also be found. The amount of earth around the hillock may be a nuisance in lawn areas, where they can interfere with mowing.

Queen ants that may come in from elsewhere are likely to be killed by the ants from your own nests, for by despatching this new queen they are helping to maintain their own existence. If you just allow for what little effect they do have, it will be enough. They are more of a help than a hindrance.

Not that many people know how many kinds of snake there are in the UK. Whilst most of us are familiar with the two main ones, the adder or viper, and the grass snake, the third one is relatively unknown – the smooth snake.

The adder may be found almost anywhere in the UK, but the grass snake prefers a slightly warmer climate and tends to dwell in the southern parts of the country. The smooth snake confines itself mainly to the southern counties. They all feed on more or less the same diet of small mammals, birds, frogs, lizards and newts and similar sized creatures.

They tend to hibernate from around the end of October through until mid-spring, when it becomes warm enough for them to move around and hunt. You will find them in the long grass, in or under the heavy undergrowth of most hedges or bushes, or actually in the pond, if you have one, for they are all excellent swimmers.

The adder is the only one who gives a painful or venomous bite, but people rarely suffer more than just the pain of the initial attack. And before you seek to exact revenge on this or any of the others please remember that all snakes are protected by law. You are not allowed to kill them.

Hopefully, this chapter has opened one or two eyes to exactly what can and does happen in the garden. Whatever you can do to help out in these hard times will be appreciated, not only by the garden wildlife, but also by you when you get to view the results of your (and their) efforts.

Tips & Wrinkles

THIS LIST IS not a "be-all and end-all" of lunar gardening philosophy by any means, but over the years it has become an invaluable guide with an extremely helpful set of hints which, if adopted, will help to achieve that extra edge to your finished holding.

Aeration

Where possible, and for the best results, try to aerate the soil when the Moon is ascending. Earth and soil tends to break up much more easily when the Moon is descending.

Bees and Wasps

If you have to do any work near where a swarm of bees or wasps have their nests, make sure the Sun is in a Fire sign and the Moon is in an Air sign. The insects will allow you to do what you want, without giving you cause for worry. They will not tolerate any interference when the Moon passes through a Water sign.

Calendar

The weekly, monthly and seasonal calendar we enjoy here in the UK is sun or solar based. The astrological system that the vast majority of astrologers generally tend to use is moon or lunar based. The two methods will never meet in our life time, although just occasionally the moon phases do seem to connect with the solar year for a short while. This tends to happen quite often in January when the first day of the year often coincides with the first quarter phase of the Moon. But that is all it is – pure coincidence.

Cleaning

The use of insecticides, disinfectants, DDT and all the many other proprietary cleaners, has been having a devastating effect on the natural life of plants and animals just about everywhere. When cleaning out in the open, in the greenhouse, the garden shed or even indoors, do try to use natural cleaners wherever possible because these new cleaners are creating an imbalance on nature in general

It may seem quite strange to you (at least, until you try them), but ordinary baby-wipes, as bought in supermarkets, will clean many a surface far better than most dirt removers will – and they don't do any damage.

When you think about it, they are made to clean a baby so they can't do any harm, can they?

Composting

It helps to have a proper compost bin to hold any and all organic waste you can recycle from the kitchen and garden, because once it has rotted down, you can use it as a base for mulch. Never put what might seem to be dead weeds in, for they have a habit of coming alive again very easily. Hedgerow clippings, raw vegetables, fruit peelings, small bits of cardboard, ash from a bonfire or a garden barbecue, are all acceptable.

Try not to use cooked meats or animal faeces for it will attract rats. Avoid newspapers and magazines, for they do not rot down very well.

Try to start your compost when the Moon is in Scorpio, although Cancer or Pisces will do. The mixture should be "turned" when the Moon is waning in the last quarter, in Aries, Leo or Aquarius.

Cucumbers

The best tasting cucumbers should be sown under glass or in the greenhouse in February, when the Moon is in her first quarter, or the first ten degrees or so of Taurus. They really are worth the effort.

Cuttings

There are slightly different rules for taking cuttings between indoor and outdoor plants, but it would be best to do this in the first or second quarters, when the Moon is in Cancer, Scorpio and Pisces – pot straightaway using the same rules.

Deadheading

The expression is quite well known, but few people know exactly why we use it. Flowering plants produce seeds, but once their blossoms die, they may well be left alone or eventually fall away of their own accord. You can achieve more blossoms by removing the dying or dead head, because this fools the plant and it will actually produce even more. Thus, deadheading is the best way of getting the most from your flowers.

Fertiliser

It is best to fertilise as the Moon passes though the fruitful signs, that is, Taurus, Cancer, Scorpio or Pisces. For the best results, always use a chemically based fertiliser in the first or second quarters but an organic one in the third or fourth quarters.

Fences

Repair, replace or create new fences in a waning Moon preferably when she is in Taurus, Leo or Aquarius. Virgo or Capricorn may also be considered or, alternatively, on the day the Moon becomes new, irrespective of the sign she occupies at the time. If created when the Moon is in a Water sign, Cancer, Scorpio or Pisces, the wood will rot more quickly.

First Aid – Indoors

If you do not have any indoor plants you might like to consider having at least one pot of Aloe Vera available because of its remarkable healing properties in the event of sting, scald, burn, or a small cut. This is widely recommended by gardeners and herbalists alike.

First Aid – Outdoors

Always try to have a few ordinary English marigolds growing somewhere in the garden because in the event of a sting, scald, burn or a small cut you will be able to rub the leaf of this plant on the affected area. This part of the plant contains calendula, which will instantly soothe the wounded area until you can get at something better – always assuming you will need it, after using this leaf.

Fish

If you have fish in your garden pond, the water should be at least 60 to 70 centimetres deep. This ensures the bottom part remains cool in hot weather and, in the winter, ice is less likely to form. Fish are ruled by the Moon or Neptune, and fish ponds by Pisces.

If or when introducing new fish into your pond, lay the bag in which they come on the water surface for a short while to allow the temperatures to even up. Untie the bag and allow them to leave the bag when they want. It doesn't pay to be too pushy with them at this stage.

Flowers

The best-looking flowers should always be planted out when the Moon is in her first quarter, in Libra.

Fountain

Should you have a pond of any reasonable size, do think seriously about adding a small fountain or waterfall. Duckweed will not form on moving water. Fountains are ruled by the Moon and/or Venus, while waterfalls are influenced most by Pisces.

Freezers

In these modern times there are many gardeners who "fool" their seeds into thinking that is it the right time of the year for that seed to now grow. They do this by putting them into a container in the freezer until they want to use them. Now – this is not only clever, it works. Try it.

Greenhouse Heating

With power costing what it does these days, leave a large candle alight in a safe position in the greenhouse overnight, but with the door closed, of course. This is often sufficient enough protection from any frost outside getting in – and it is a much cheaper exercise too.

Guttering

It is quite a large task to clean the guttering and drainpipes. So, start the work when the Moon is on the wane. In the long run, the clearance work does seem to last that little bit less.

Hands

Of necessity, hands get dirty after a session in any part of any garden. When you start to wash them, always use cold water first. This will cause the pores to close and help get rid of the grime much more easily. Once most of the dirt seems to have gone, then use warm – not hot water, and your hands will respond beautifully.

Hanging Baskets

Anything planted placed into a hanging basket of any kind will dry out very quickly, no matter how well you manage to try to keep it moist. If you must have one then line it well first and put an old soup plate or something similar at the very bottom to catch any moisture. Use a better than average moist compost. Hanging baskets are ruled by Venus.

If you like herbs but do not have the ground space to grow them separately then use hanging baskets and put a couple or so in each. As long as you attend to the needs of the individual herb, they make excellent places in which to be raised.

Hoses – New and Old

When buying a new hose, measure the full distance of what you will need from the (outside?) tap you normally use, to the extreme end of the garden. Now add around six to ten metres or so extra for getting around those awkward little areas and corners, so that the new hose will never kink causing those irritating losses of pressure that can occur at such times.

If the old hose won't connect properly to anything, think before you get rid of it, because this can be a most helpful piece of gardening equipment when used the right way. Cut both ends cleanly and bury the hose just under the surface and at the side, from one end of the garden to the other (or as far as it will go), without trying to join it up to any existing connection.

You may now run an electricity cable (or cables) through the old hose to the bottom of the garden, where most folk have their garden shed or greenhouse, and enjoy a safe and well-protected power cable connection to either or both of them.

Alternatively, put the right connectors on each end of the old hose and, when you want to water the garden, all you have to do is connect it to your new hose without having to un-reel the replacement unnecessarily. These two ideas save time and effort all round.

Houseplants

Strictly speaking, there are no such things as house plants but in general whatever you do plant to keep indoors should be planted in the first or second quarter when the Moon is in Taurus, Cancer, Libra, Scorpio or Pisces. If you do not like indoor plants, you might like to consider having at least one pot of Aloe Vera available because of its remarkable healing properties in the event of burns, minor cuts or insect bites.

Ladders

Sooner or later you will need to use a ladder (ruled by Gemini) to go up just a couple of steps or all the way up the side of your house. To ensure a firm base, especially if you have to stand the ladder in earth, place both of the ladder's "feet" in empty paint tins. This will ensure the ladder will not sink in to the soil or slip away. When the Moon is in Gemini is the best time for their use.

Lawns

To make the most of the appearance, not only of your lawn, but the whole garden as well, you should mow in the second quarter to stimulate growth. To help slow things down a bit more, one should mow in the fourth quarter. Lawns are ruled by Venus. Attend to a lawn when the Moon is in Taurus or Libra for the best results. It is worth noting here that a long lawn with equal sides will make the viewer automatically look to the furthest point, thus making it seem longer than it actually is. A round lawn makes a garden seem larger, while an "L" shaped affair, where you cannot see it all, creates a small mystery. People will want to see more.

Leaking Hoses

Occasionally, you may experience a small hole in a hose that seems to defy all efforts to repair it. A small piece of wood like a toothpick should be pushed into the hole – but not too far. Thoroughly wet the area so that the wood expands. Put a small piece of sellotape over the tear first, then properly seal the whole area with a tight band of duck-tape.

Leaves

One or two gardeners reserve a small area in their flower section for a display of plants that produce coloured leaves only. If carefully grown with the right effort, the end result can be quite definitely stunning.

Mole Hills

Unsightly at the best of times, these little growths not only spoil the view, they also offend. There are two remedies to offset their re-appearance. Cut an onion in half and place one of the halves face down in the hole. Alternatively, put a small amount of used cat litter into the top of the hole.

Mulch

Mulch is a kind of protective blanket put over healthy soil and is created from inorganic or organic material. Organic mulch, which includes grass clippings, leaves and small pieces of wood, tends to decompose fairly quickly. Gravel and black plastic are examples of inorganic mulches that do not always break down and does not have to be replaced too often.

Grass clippings tend to form a thick pad through which water may not always be able to permeate easily. One should take care not to use clippings from lawns that have been treated with an herbicide. Gravel pebbles or small stones are much more permanent and are quite effective against weeds. You can use newspaper but it has to be made firm so that it does not blow away at the slightest breeze.

Small bits of wood are usually created when you work at odd jobs in the garden. Bark from trees is liable to be found almost anywhere and, for as long as it reasonably fresh, it will be good to use, but it performs best when mixed in with compost or well-aged manure. Mulching is best carried out when the Moon is waxing and in Air or Earth signs.

Mushrooms

Start mushrooms in the first or second quarters ideally when the Moon is in Cancer. Always try to pick them at the Full Moon – they always seem to taste that little bit nicer.

Netting

You should always spread thin netting over the top of any pond and allow for about 10cm height above the water level. If you have fish, this will help to keep the heron away. It will also keep leaves and other debris from falling into the water. It will afford a degree of shelter for other bird life and any small animal to visit and drink in safety. This also allows for frogs, toads and newts to freely move about as well.

Ornamental Grass

To be really different, why not devote a small area to a collection of coloured grass? Start them off in April when the Moon is in her second quarter, in Capricorn.

Paint Storage

When you have used the paint in a tin or other type of container, make sure the lid is quite firmly in place before putting it where you want to keep it, but turn the container upside down. When you turn the holder back up the right way, the paint will be ready for use because the thick skin that almost always forms on the top will now be on the bottom. Paint and painters are ruled by Venus.

Paths and Paving

If you feel like a change put in a small bend (or bends) into a straight path. Alternatively, if your pathway is straight then create a curve. A cleverly planted bush at such a point is very effective and the change to the appearance to your garden can be quite dramatic as well, becoming a talking point for visitors. Although paths and pathways are ruled by Mercury, this work is best undertaken when the Moon is waning, preferably in Capricorn, but never when she is in Cancer, or the work will not last long.

Pests

To destroy pests (or weeds) you use the fourth quarter when the Moon is in a barren sign like Aries, Gemini, Leo or Aquarius. Instead of buying an expensive spray, follow this homemade idea. Fill a reasonably sized mug with sugar. Place in a saucepan and add a quarter mugful of water, and bring it all to the boil. Let the mixture cool and settle. Dilute it by about four parts ordinary water to one part of this new solution, then spray where it is needed.

Ponds

Ponds generally are ruled by the Moon and, to start one from scratch, begin when she is passing through Cancer, Scorpio or Pisces. Double check the garden position you have chosen, for too much sunlight is unhelpful and may cause an influx of algae. Use a proper spirit level to ensure the finished article won't have what seems like an irregular surface to it.

For best results use a dark coloured good quality material for lining, for it will not reflect the light so easily and you won't want to have to do it all again after five or six years. Tap water is not always good for a refill. Always place a pump and or filters where you can get at them quickly if or when they either go wrong or need to be cleaned and/or serviced. Pond life can and will suffer if a pump or a filter is out of action for too long because you cannot get at them quickly enough.

Pruning

All pruning work is best carried out when the Moon is waning in Scorpio, but Capricorn will yield very good results, for this position will help the cuts to heal more quickly.

Safety First

Never leave keys in any lock, even if you are still in the house. If they can be seen through a window or a glass pane in the door, a thief will have all they want in one fell swoop. They will break the glass, take the keys and, if you have a spare car key on the ring as well – you have lost your car too.

There will always be bits of hose lengths over, no matter how hard you try to use what is left. Don't throw any of it away. Cut up the old hose into lengths to match your saws and any other sharp edge equipment you may have. Cut these small pieces lengthwise and slip them over all your sharp hard edges for added safety.

Salads

Think twice before you plant or sow vegetable salads. Never plant everything all at once, or it will all be ready at the same time. Instead, sow a couple of rows of this or that every so often and you will be assured of a more continuous supply. You can start to sow small salad ingredients as early as January if you have a heated greenhouse and use a frame or a hotbed. If you like spring onions and cannot wait until they are ready, chives make an excellent alternative.

Shelf Space

Here is a clever way to double the use of your shelves in the garden shed or greenhouse. Save empty screw-lid jars. Make a small hole in the lid and screw it to the underside of a shelf, put whatever you want in the jar and screw the jar to the lid. The result is a better and fuller use of your shelves. Make the necessary adjustments if you have metal shelves.

Slugs

These creatures do a lot of damage even when whatever you have planted is under cloches. Use slug pellets or good slug bait amply distributed wherever there are signs of their existence. Initially, a line of ordinary household salt will stop them but the end result can be rather messy.

Alternatively dig little holes in the area and place used small plastic cups or the bottom of a plastic bottle into the hole. When the slug falls in, simply remove them and put them in an open pathway. The birds will love you for their surprise meals. If you don't like this idea, then you destroy what you find.

Snow

For as long as any snowfall covers your garden, and that includes all of the plants – not the trees, of course, then your growths will be largely unaffected. However, if the snow does not cover the plant then frost is likely to attack what is showing. Take the necessary action if this should happen in your area.

When you begin to clear freshly fallen snow from paths or drives use salt and/or small grit, but sweep it on to a hard surface in the garden, not a plant area or the lawn, for it will kill the growths underneath.

Spraying

The spraying of insecticides, weed killers and similar materials should be carried out during a waning Moon in a barren sign – Aries, Gemini, Leo or Aquarius. Often, it pays to carry out this sort of task in the early evening, for many different types of pests materialise after the Sun goes down.

Squirrels

It is always a pleasure to watch these lovely little creatures gambolling about, but they are pests. If you have bird feeders on poles, you may have to move them to where the squirrel cannot get at them. If you really want to upset them, pile as much grease as you can up and down the poles. After leaping on and sliding down, they soon give up and go elsewhere. For extra safety put largish wooden boards above or under the actual bird feeder. If they do manage to get that far, they won't be able to get past this blockade.

Transplanting

Transplants are best carried out when the Moon is waxing, passing preferably through Cancer, although Taurus, Libra, Scorpio and Pisces produce good results as well.

Water Butt

In the event of drought conditions applying, there are several ways of conserving what does drop out of the sky – especially in April. Kill two birds with one stone here because you will be conserving pure rain water in a water butt connected to the downpipe from your gutter. The butt will have to be raised up so that you can fill your watering can from the tap supplied. Wrap an old stocking around the bottom end of the down pipe and this will catch any unwanted debris from going into the water. There is also a saving here, when there is a lot of rain about. Tap water isn't too well-liked by a lot of different plant life, for many seem to flourish better when they drink in rain water as an alternative. Water butts are ruled by the Moon, preferably when she is in Cancer, but Scorpio and Pisces may also be considered.

Watering

Despite much advice to the contrary, do try to avoid watering your patch too late in the evenings. You see, when you use your hose, you will also water the leaves of your plants and, if they cannot dry out overnight, they may start to decay. Rotting leaves can cause a plant to die, so water gently instead in the early hours – especially at the roots of new or young plants.

Also, try to avoid watering during the middle of the day, because water tends to evaporate and the leaves will end up scorched. Oh, and get rid of the sprinkler because it really is most wasteful. Water when the Moon is in any of the Water signs, that is, Cancer, Scorpio or Pisces.

When drought situations arise, water the garden as suggested, but you can safely ignore the lawn in favour of freshly sown plant life or vegetables. The lawn will come back to life a few days after the next reasonable rainfall, but fresh plants and vegetables require careful nursing at such times.

Weather Considerations

In spite of the big chapter on weather elsewhere in this book, in certain rural areas it has been claimed that it does not seem to rain so much when the Moon passes through Taurus, Virgo or Capricorn. When tasks involving Water signs are required, it can sometimes coincide with a rainfall that makes it rather difficult in which to work comfortably. In such circumstances, it is quite safe to wait until the Moon transits an Earth sign.

Weeds

Weeds want as much water as your ordinary plants, if not more so, in some cases. This competition should be stopped. So, the instant you see a weed, remove it immediately, not in an hour or so or tomorrow – but now! Weeds are ruled by Pluto. Weeding is best done when the Moon is in Scorpio, but any time will do, in most cases.

Wheelbarrows

If your garden is large enough for you to need one, then always buy one that has a ball for a wheel because it will manoeuvre so much better over almost all surfaces. Try to ensure you buy one when the Moon is passing through Capricorn or Aquarius.

PART TWO

January

WHEN THE WEATHER is a little too rough to venture out, spend a little of your indoor time going through all your garden machinery and tools. Sort out what you can sharpen or service yourself, and ship off all those you can't manage. Do any of these things need to be replaced, or could you add one or two items to your collection? Only you can answer that one.

Because of all sorts of weather conditions likely at this time of the year, it is almost impossible to know exactly where to start. If the opportunity presents itself, I would suggest that it would be more than helpful if you could sweep over your lawn with a besom broom or, if you haven't got one, a reasonably stiff-bristled version will do. Dead grass, leaves or anything else for that matter, can be quite damaging and worm casts are dreadful. However, their excretions do at least show to remind you that the gardener does have some help.

Once this has been done, serve the lawn with a top-dressing of fine soil and work it well into the turf. Don't just let it lie there on the top of the grass, for if it gets blown away it won't do the job you intended. Work it into the turf with a flat edge of a tool of some kind, a shovel or the back of a flat iron rake will do admirably.

It never hurts to run a brush or just a long piece of wood along hedges to give them a bit of shake-up. This will remove moisture, dead litter and whatever else may be lodged in them. Don't go mad, but a few minutes spent doing this will help to reap a good reward.

Good gardeners will want to get on with digging in and cultivating fresh patches. Now, although the ground may be hard because of the frost, or even just the cold, the wise gardener would have first covered the area with a large piece of old carpeting or something heavy or similar, to ensure the ground underneath did not firm up too much because of the winter cold. In an unheated greenhouse, all you need do is cover your plants with sheets of newspaper overnight. But remember to remove them during the daylight hours.

January is an excellent time for the gardener to plan out an herb garden. Not all people do this but it should be remembered that, because these plants have such a multitude of uses and purposes, they are worth considering. Once your planning is completed and your plants are sown out, they need very little maintenance other than the usual tasks associated with all plants, of course.

As a rule, it is wise to plant herbs in such a way that they will not be overly disturbed by wind and, if possible, so that that they may also have a fair amount of sunlight. Almost all herbs thrive in sunlight – very few dislike the light and they will be individually mentioned each month, when and where it is necessary to do so.

It is worth considering that if this should be your first foray in to growing herbs, then once you have decided which you are going to grow and where you are going to put them, you should order your seeds from an established or specialist herb nursery centre.

So, back to the garden; sooner or later, a few bulbs will start to show where you have daffodils, hyacinths and tulips growing. Use a small fork, a hand one is ideal, and lightly prick over the ground but not too forcibly, just enough to get at a few hardy weeds and to give your new growths a better chance by aerating the ground.

Give your greenhouse a good airing. Clean it through, water gently; change the soil where needed and look out for decaying bits and pieces which should be removed immediately. Clean the glass or plastic, oil the door hinges and the windows. After this, bulbs may be brought inside. Some cuttings may be taken, like carnations and chrysanthemums, along with a whole host of other possible root cuttings to suit.

Some gardeners will plant out a few small items even this early in the year, like small salad plants, for example. Other useful plantings may be made of mustard and cress, radishes and small lettuces which should be started off in frames. Elsewhere, plant potatoes and onions, a few carrots, leeks perhaps and french beans, mushrooms and endive.

Flowers should also take up your attention about now. Some replanting will be necessary and remember that when you change the soil in your pots make sure the replacement really is fresh – try not to use old soil that has been doing nothing for a few months. This might well mean a visit to a local Garden Centre but, of course, this is where you can also stock up on new seeds and mull over a few new ideas you might want to try.

Plant herbaceous perennials and a few sweet peas under cloches, and have a look at the state of some of your fruit trees and bushes while you are at it. Check the grease bands where you have used them and find where it looks as though fresh material should be applied, because now is an excellent time.

Prune and spray whatever looks as though it might benefit from such an exercise. Almost all fruit trees should be sprayed and vines will respond well to a gentle pruning touch here and there While looking at the fruits, if you should have any cuttings made in the autumn of last year like currants or gooseberries, they might need to be firmed up because of the action of frost or even snow, if you had some of that as well.

It might be a tad early, but if you have young fruit bushes, or trees for that matter, you would do well to take some action against the action of birds because, for them, food is at a premium this month and they will treat themselves to the young buds. There are many different ways of preventing this, but the best idea that has always proved itself is to cover the smaller bushes and trees with fine netting.

It does not have to be left there for too long – eight to nine weeks at the most. Should you have fresh, young newly planted raspberries and blackcurrants, they need to be pruned well. Cut them back quite low, to not less than 15 centimetres for the raspberries, but a little less for the blackcurrants.

If we return to the greenhouse now and you have a chance for a good clean-up, you should begin to heat the place to around 17° or 20° centigrade (around 62° to 68° fahrenheit) in order to get some of your flower plantings under way. Flowers sown now like antirrhinums, gloxinias and begonias, will all do well.

If you have the time, try to take a look at your pathways and their edges. Repair and renew where you can and, while you are at it, this would be an excellent time to re-turf and patch unsightly parts of your lawns.

Again, and because of your local bird and animal life, it would be a wise step to cover this work with a fine netting, until you see the young shoots growing and your path patching has recovered. When anything looks different or fresh, animal life will always investigate, and that's how all your efforts can sometimes come to nothing.

The work listed here, to be undertaken during January, is far from complete and is meant as a general guide only. In the following paragraphs, where it is suggested you try to time your efforts with the phase and position of the Moon, is not complete either. Because it isn't mentioned in either category does not mean you should not carry out such tasks.

ASTROLOGICAL TIMING

During January the Moon will become void-of-course several times, something that occurs fairly regularly every month and, although such an event may not last too long at times there are a few occasions when it is advisable to not carry out any work that will have any long-term basis to it. As a rule, the shorter periods are reasonably harmless but when the Moon becomes void–of-course for longer spells, gardeners should try to avoid starting anything new or something quite radical.

When the Moon is in Aries, it is better to turn to the more mundane matters of gardening. Have a small bonfire so that you can really destroy bits and pieces considered noxious. Keep the ashes for later use elsewhere in your garden. Bonfire ashes are very helpful when it comes to making some of your own fresh fertiliser, always provided there is nothing left alive in it.

Now is also a very good time to give all your tools and cutting equipment a good once-over – especially the electric bits and pieces. If you can manage it, give hedges a clean-up. This is best done by running a stick of wood or a broom handle along them. This loosens much of what shouldn't be there and allows you to have a much easier clean-up afterwards.

The Moon in Taurus is about the best time to put out a few early salad plants. Mustard and cress, lettuce and radish will all grow well in frames. Even a few leeks, onions and French beans will grow nicely if put in carefully now. At this time of the year, the Moon in Taurus is always a productive time for gardeners. For example, if you have the space, you could force some rhubarb and even sea-kale outdoors but keep an eye on the weather, for that will condition what you can or cannot do.

Also, at this time of the year, it is really important to keep lawns as clear as you can and, if you do have the time work in a light dressing of soil. This will help stimulate growth as the weather eases up and temperatures start to increase a bit.

Hopefully, it is about now that you will spot a few bulbs begin to show where you have daffodils, hyacinths and tulips growing. Take a small hand-sized fork and prick lightly over the areas, not too hard now, but just enough to take out the hardier weeds. This will help to give your new growths a better chance once you have aerated their ground.

The Moon in Cancer encourages all manner of growths, so change the soil where you feel it will be needed the most. Put out a few sweet peas under cloches, run a practised eye over your bulb beds and prick out where needed.

The Moon in Leo, and then Virgo in January, encourages normal work, so clear away debris that always seems to gather in all sorts of odd spots in any garden. Dig over new patches if the weather allows and get ready for all the tasks that will need to be carried out in February.

Well, when the Moon is in the rather fruitful sign of Libra, it will be a good time to prune fruit. Peach trees and apricots need to be looked at, and then you can move on to the apples and the pears. While you are at it, give any grease bands on the stems and trunks a look, to make sure they are still effective and renew where needed.

After this, you should move on to any fruit bush plants – gooseberries and red and white currants.

These early days of the year may be a good time to see what ought to be done as a matter of priority. For example, a touch of oil on the hinges of the doors and windows in the greenhouse and garden shed will not come amiss.

Some tidying up is almost always needed after the Christmas and New Year break and quite a few plants could do with a change of soil, perhaps with a little extra watering here and there. Therefore, as the Moon travels through Scorpio, then Sagittarius and Capricorn, use the period to lift and dispose of dead plants, for the room you gain will allow you to bring in fresh bulbs and/or cuttings from other plants.

When the Moon is in Capricorn, it is always a good time to ease back and take the time to have a good look around, so that you can plan with a more general common-sense approach to the way everything looks. Sweep the lawn thoroughly, with a besom broom if you have one. Sweep off all the worm casts and note the fresh ones, for they will tell you how healthy the soil is. And, of course, the amount of fresh casts will tell you how many of nature's little helpers you do have in your lawn.

Clear away dead leaves and anything else that shouldn't be there. Use the same tactics on other grassy places, clear up paths and driveways, root out weeds and really clean all outside drains, preferably with hot water, once you have removed anything that might have been clogging them up.

Once the Moon moves into Aquarius will be an ideal period in which to put out a few sweet peas under cloches. Check the bulb beds and prick out anywhere you feel would be best or is needed. There will be precious little to harvest in any way, but you could spend time checking the condition(s) of what you do have coming along for later use.

If the weather is reasonable, a few green sprouts may begin to be showing, even at this early stage. However, if it is still cold, improve aeration a little where you can, for this will help keep down the moss and weeds.

The Moon in Pisces will take some extra effort and energy with really getting into the nitty-gritty of early gardening. Early apricot, nectarine and peach trees will flourish better in summer if you treat them right. Keep new trees in a warm greenhouse for a while, and they will begin to respond.

The Pisces Moon also favours starting a few fresh vegetables for harvesting later in the year. Start carrots, peas, potatoes and even a few tomatoes sown now should be ready by late May. Some flowers may be also be sown out now – antirrhinums, begonias and gloxinias will do well and, if you have the room, bring any new shrubs and roses into the warmer air of your greenhouse, to allow them become a little tougher.

February

THE WEATHER OUGHT to start to ease around now and, on those occasions where you can get out, it is time to prepare spring seed beds and other similar activities. Roses need to be planted this month but not if there is any frost, otherwise you will have to do so under glass or in the greenhouse. Also, sow lilies and other plants under glass.

All bulbs should be planted out in mild weather, where possible, and alpines should be looked at, for they will need to be firmed up where they may have been loosened by frost. The same goes for any heather plants, as well as your fruit bushes or trees that may have been planted out earlier.

A few pruning exercises around now won't hurt, especially those by a pond, if you have one. Concentrate on all rose and standard bushes but leave tea roses until much later in the year. When you cut back, keep a look out for any damaged dead growths. If unsure, cut the shoot back to between 12–15 centimetres. This will ensure a good display later in the year.

While we are looking at flowers, please note that gladiola corms will flower well when they are allowed to sprout in the greenhouse. Lily bulbs, sweet peas and pinks, along with some half-hardy annuals may also be looked at. If already established, take a few cuttings of alpine plants.

A few adventurous gardeners have filbert and cobnut bushes in their garden. At some time this month a few small red flowers will appear. Around the same period, a few catkin-like growths will also appear. Now is the time to be very careful how you approach the task of pruning of these plants. Make sure you also do away with any unsightly or wrongly growing branches.

The idea of the bush is for it to look like one, so you may have to cut more away than you might like in some places, but it won't hurt. Now also is a good time to attend to walnut trees, if you have them.

February is also a very good month in which to renew or start a small rock garden. Collect some eight or nine largish stones, more if you have the space. Lay them out where you want, ensure you have a good drainage run and always choose a sunny spot for this area, never in the shade or under trees, for rock gardens thrive in the light. Put in place plenty of good fresh soil, peat and compost around them and plant out your alpines as you will.

Good gardeners will go all out now to complete their digging and trench making. Break down any rough ground, because once this is out of the way you can concentrate more easily on getting new plants to grow. February is always a busy sowing and planting period, whichever way you turn.

Weeding and clearing away unnecessary debris and rubbish is almost always a bind, but it has to be done. As you are carrying out the work, you will see where the early slugs and other pests are raiding the good stuff (to them that is), so then you can lay out the necessary repellents and slug pellets where needed.

While you are performing these tasks, you may see squirrels visiting, to see what they can get. If you have bird feeders on poles, you may have to remove them to where the squirrel cannot get at them. If you really want to upset them, pile as much grease as you can up and down the poles. After leaping on to them and sliding down a couple of times, they soon give up and go elsewhere. The expression on their little faces is an absolute joy to behold.

You may well spend a lot of time in the greenhouse and, if so, you will be able to gauge when to aerate the place, without allowing in too much cold. Watch out for high winds coming through the open door or windows.

It doesn't hurt to keep water in here either, for it will be a tad warmer than outside. Your plants will appreciate that touch. While working in the greenhouse, do remember to pot out annuals that you may have sown in the late summer last year, for flowering later this year. If you place them singly in 10–12 centimetre high pots, then place them on the shelves, this will encourage them to become quite strong.

Early vegetables can now be safely sown under cloches. A small selection of a few broad beans will flourish, preferably if you space them out at about 5–6 centimetres apart, rather than just throw the seed into the soil willy-nilly. In the greenhouse you may sow cauliflower, peas and lettuce. A few cucumbers sown now will reap out nicely later in the year.

Other vegetables that may be started during this month are parsnips, which should be sown out at about 20–25 centimetres apart. Early beetroot started now will be ready for the middle of June. These don't require so much space, as the seeds are larger by comparison than with most other vegetables. Early celery, a few shallots, along with a selection of cabbage, broccoli and even a few early parsnips, should do well.

For those who like them, Jerusalem artichokes can also be planted out about 30–35 centimetres apart. As these plants can grow to the height of a man they will create a certain amount of shade and act as wind-break when they do come to maturity – useful if looking for a temporary shady area for other things.

Another sowing of main crop tomatoes, planted out separately in very small pots – about 5 or 6 centimetres or so, will suffice here. If it is reasonably warm, there is no reason why a few early turnips can't be planted out in the garden. Only sow a few at a time to start with and place them about 25–30 centimetres or so apart. Once they are under way you may repeat this every three weeks or so until mid-summer. This method creates a series of fresh young plants as against the chance of some old tough ones, possibly spoiling a meal.

Toward the end of the month, and when you have the time, hedges may be added to with young plants, but preferably when it is mild and dry. Try to keep them fairly frost free for a short while, until they root and settle in properly.

This is also a good time to trim back any overgrown parts of hedges and it wouldn't hurt to have another sweep of the lawn and then aerate it as best you can. The essential thing is to remove the worm casts as often as possible. Moss or weed growths should be treated now to minimise the problems they could bring later on.

The work listed here to be carried out during February, is not complete by any means and has been compiled as a general guide only. The following paragraphs, where it is suggested you try to time your efforts with the phase and position of the Moon, is not complete either. Because it isn't mentioned in either category does not mean you should not carry out such tasks.

ASTROLOGICAL TIMING

Early February is always a good time to make friends with the robins (and any other animal life) that are constant visitors to your garden. They are always there – all you have to is to start digging and they will come close by to spot what you will unearth. If a worm or other small animal life should surface, stop to allow the robin or other creature to have his or her feed. If you do this now, they will keep an eye open for you and, the moment you appear, then so will they. Now, you can all enjoy your garden.

During the February period, and when the Moon is in Aries, you should take the time to give all your tools and equipment a once-over. Clean them and make sure they are all usable, before you start the next task.

The Taurus Moon is an ideal time to sow a small amount of early celery under a frame. Next month might be a tad better, but what you start now will see you with plenty of this vegetable, nice and fresh, by September.

At about this time, it wouldn't hurt to sow more main crop tomatoes along with a handful of early turnips. Plant out potatoes and some early parsley in a sheltered area. Where possible, plant out last year's autumn sown onions, if the soil will allow it. A few more French beans for successional growth won't hurt now.

A Gemini Moon doesn't favour any new sowing or planting at all. Clear away debris wherever you see it – and that means now, not later, as this really is not a favourable time for proper gardening as such. Sweep pathways and drives well and edge all of them properly.

Don't forget your hedges either. Tap all of your hedge tops again with a piece of wood or even the handle of a broom or other tool and then clear away underneath them. It is important to now destroy all unwanted weeds, pests and other growths, preferably in a small bonfire.

During February when the Moon starts to pass through Cancer, plant and sow a fairly diverse amount of different plant life. A few early turnips, placed about 20-25 centimetres away from each other. Once you are satisfied with their progress, by all means continue to do this every few weeks or so, until early to midsummer and you will be able to enjoy a regular supply of good fresh plants, rather than some old and probably tough varieties you may well have grown earlier.

You should also put just a few sowings of main crop tomatoes in fairly small pots and, if you have the space, make a sowing of broad beans under glass, along with a few lettuces, peas and cauliflowers.

The greenhouse will need some attention so that when the Moon traverses through Leo especially if in the middle of the month (or at any other time really) you can throw the door(s) wide open and do the same for the windows because, the fresher the air you usher in the better.

However, don't overdo it too much because it will probably be a lot warmer in than out, and you don't want to be lowering the temperature just yet. Keep a small supply of water in the greenhouse, because it will be warmer than outside, and your plants will appreciate it.

While the Moon is in Virgo, it is a good time to pot out all the annuals you sowed last year, for flowering this year. Put them into larger than average single pots but keep them on the shelves for a while. If you have any, check filbert and/or cobnut bushes for the small red flowers or the follow up of the catkin type of growth. Prune them very carefully and don't overdo it. Frankly, if you aren't sure, then leave it alone altogether.

The few days or so when the Moon passes through Libra and then Scorpio will give you lots of time to attend to your flowers. Start to force roses and other flowering shrubs and, if you still have any room, now is the time to put more flowers into the greenhouse.

Achimenes may also be started. Put the tubers into shallow boxes, as against pots, and cover them with a slightly sandy mixture, and water well. You may also prune flowering shrubs, but please be careful, they are rather prone to the vagaries of the weather just now.

If the Moon is in her last quarter, especially if she is in Scorpio and then Sagittarius, sow a few cucumbers for an early crop. The phase of the Moon is not so important at this stage, but her placing is. Wait a day or so and then plant out a few shallots and onions, provided the soil is reasonably receptive. Sow them about 20-25 centimetres apart. They will need to be firmly pushed well down and lightly covered. Continue as you see fit, but beware of those surprising frosts that don't always announce themselves until they arrive.

During February, as with all months, the Moon occasionally becomes void-of-course. Just remember that, at such times, it is best to not start anything important or long-lasting, because the chances are you may well have to start all over again if you do

After Sagittarius the Moon will start to pass through Capricorn – a good time to look at where the herb part of the garden has been placed. Divide and replant chives, put in some garlic and clear away any unnecessary growths that might hinder them in any way. Move on to the salad and vegetable patches and sow a few fresh radishes, some early spring cabbages, artichokes and a small amount of parsnips.

For as long as the weather holds out, it won't hurt to sow a relatively early selection of freesia, verbena and half-hardy annuals – marigolds, dianthus, dahlias, lobelias and so on. If you have the time, feel free to re-pot ferns, if you have any, of course.

The Moon will move on into Aquarius after this. Where possible, keep to ordinary jobs around any part of your garden. For example, and where possible, dig over new patches for later planting and sowing. Find the time to check out whatever bird-feeders you may have. It won't hurt to re-grease the poles that keep them up, for this will keep enquiring and ever-hungry squirrels at bay.

As the Moon pushes on through Pisces, take the opportunity to look at your rock garden and fish pond – if you have one. Ensure the drainage method for the rock garden is still intact and working properly. Clear away any small blockages that may have been created by the winter. Use a strong small pronged rake and take away as much of the old earth as you can. Mix up some fresh soil with peat and compost to cover the new areas that have been left a tad bare.

It is most important to drain off as much of the old water in the pond as you can. Clean off any surface bits and pieces that ought not to be there and then slowly re-fill the pond. The best way to do this is to lay the hose pipe along the top and allow fresh new water to slowly bring it all back up to a normal level again.

March

MUCH OF THE colder weather should have gone by now and we ought to be able to start to enjoy spring-like weather – hopefully. Although spring doesn't actually start until the Sun enters Aries, usually on the 21st, we should be able to get quite a few of our tasks under way long before then.

The days will now start to become noticeably longer and it is important that you ensure you maintain a steady greenhouse temperature all the time. Around 14° to about 18° centigrade (roughly 58° to about 65° Fahrenheit, for those who prefer the old method) should be the norm for a while. The soil may seem to be a little harder than usual and will need to be broken up, especially if you are going to rotate some of your more regular planting areas.

This is a good time to re-pot and replant growths like wall-flowers, forget-me-knots or double daisies. Break up clumps of some of your older perennials by dividing them into smaller pieces and replant using fresh soil. You will notice that succulents and cactus plants tend to drink a lot now, and will need watering more frequently and so also will any plants you have brought indoors. Some authorities also claim that carnations seem to drink more frequently about now.

March is good for planting out trees, bushes and even hedge renewal can be safely undertaken – at the right times of course. As a rule, a hedge, provided it is well placed (that is, if it is not primarily acting as a border between you and your neighbour), can often be quite useful as a windbreak, for it provides a useful shelter for all kinds of flowering shrubs and other plants.

This in itself allows you to have a colourful area here, instead of just plain green privet. March is just about the last time you can reasonably expect success from hedge planting. If you plant any later in the year the roots may not have sufficient time to become established.

Really serious attention should now be paid to all lawns as well, for turf-laying is often carried out during this period. As you work here and there, you will almost certainly see where you can clear away all manner of unwanted bits and pieces. If you are laying turf or starting a whole new lawn, this is the best time of the year to put everything into action. Borrow or hire a light roller to help press the new top into place.

All of your pathways will probably need some work on them and, if you have one, you should look at the state of your drive as well, especially if it is tarmac or of a similar type. Check all steps – even if it is only a one up. Now is the time to make everything usable and in good condition for people of all ages. If any annual weeds have returned, then use your hoe, although what you will have left may not look overly attractive, it will soon look nice again.

The vegetable section of the garden becomes very important in March. There is very little that you can't plant or sow but, probably because of the size of your particular area in most cases, you have to be selective as you move around.

During March onion sets, that is, onions that have had their growth stopped toward the end of last year, may be planted out, as can more peas, carrots, cabbage, parsnips and sprouts. Leeks from seed may be started about now, to allow you to plant out around mid-June.

While it may be a tad early in some areas, kohlrabi may be started from seed about now although April might be better if the weather is poor. If you have any, it won't hurt to plant a few early asparagus plants either. With what you have already under way, this rather widens the choice of vegetables enough for most folk.

For the salad lovers, lettuce, radish and even a few early cucumbers may be sown. Some folk have even started beetroot this month, although it is about a few weeks or so early. It isn't too late to divide and replant chives either, for they are a good substitute for onions. You could even start a little chicory in the greenhouse, for this can be eaten raw in a salad. Much depends on the weather for such things to become successful.

The flower garden begins to go quite mad about now and you do become so spoilt for choice. Of course, you won't use half what will be suggested here but you will have a wide enough range to suit most tastes. The adventurous may even stop growing one in favour of something new, for a change.

Hardy and half-hardy annuals are usually started this month and among them will almost certainly be clarkia and convolvulus. Alyssum will be a must for those who want to make their rockeries a little more colourful. Lobelia is a firm favourite, as is helianthus (preferably the small "dwarf sun-gold" variety), which does not grow to more than about 60 centimetres, as a rule.

Gypsophila, nigella or "love-in-a-mist" and begonia all have lovely early displays and give the garden some colour while you are waiting for everything else to mature. The list is virtually endless.

We may not suffer that much these days, but March winds can do a lot of damage that we don't always appreciate until we see for ourselves what has gone wrong. It is advisable to make a check of the ties you put in place earlier to secure plants to stakes and wires. Also, make sure your labels, where you may have had to use them, are still in position.

For those who have patios of any size, now is a good time to look through all the containers so that, where you deem necessary, re-pot all plants that could do with it. As you have already selected the variety of containers needed for this area, make sure that all the water drainage holes are clear to allow free flow, before you load in the fresh new soil.

If you have made arrangements to start a small herb garden, March is a good month in which to continue to work on the soil and, if you have one, use a proper seed drill for this exercise. Allow about 20 centimetres or so between plants – at least to begin with, for it isn't always easy to know how your herbs will grow. You may begin the month with sorrel, chives, some chervil, parsley and marjoram. Sow the seeds about 2–3 centimetres deep; amounts will depend on whether you want them for table use only, or to keep some back for later storage.

The work listed here for March is far from complete and has been compiled as a guide only. The following suggestions for when and what tasks to try to time your efforts with the phase and position of the Moon, is not complete either. Because it isn't mentioned in either category does not mean you should not carry out such tasks.

ASTROLOGICAL TIMING

This month the Moon could be void-of-course several times – and each time it will be for the whole day. Some of these periods only last for a few minutes or even hours. These may be taken as reasonably harmless. It is when the Moon is void–of-course for the longer time that you should try to avoid the more serious aspect of gardening, such as starting anything new or something quite radical.

When the Moon enters Aries, you may begin some simple pruning exercises which should be pursued with a good pair of secateurs. Where you are able to do so, turn over soil and remove unwanted growths. Have a bonfire so that you can properly destroy decayed, dying or dead materials that have piled up.

This can include any other debris and rubbish you have been unable to get rid of earlier. Remember to keep the ashes for later use. Once the Moon has entered Taurus, begin to work on your lawn(s), because all these kinds of grassy areas will need some sort of attention.

New lawns will, of course, require proper turf-laying and such work is best suited for about now. As you become involved with this, you will have to clear away a lot of accumulated rubbish from the winter period.

Should you have to lay turf or start a whole new lawn, this is the best time of the year to put everything into action. Borrow or hire a light roller to help press the new top into place. The vegetable garden also takes on an added importance so feel free to plant or sow just about anything at this time of the month.

Plant out more peas, parsnips, sprouts and carrots. Cauliflower and broccoli may be started in a frame, broad beans may be sown out and it won't hurt to sow a little spinach in a sheltered area. Renew or split your rhubarb corms now and put in some horseradish and early cucumbers.

The Moon pushes on into Cancer and, unless you have already started to do so, you should now start work on your hardy and half-hardy annuals. What you choose for your particular garden is entirely up to you, but don't forget your rock garden.

Put in some alyssum after a little tidy up. It doesn't take long to weed through here gently in order to clear away unwanted bits of debris that always seems to accumulate just when you don't want it.

Once the Moon begins her journey through Leo, you should widen all hoeing and weeding exercises to take in whatever else and wherever it is needed. Sweep the lawn firmly with a besom broom, clear away unwanted growths on paths, drives and their edges.

Once the Moon has passed into Virgo, it will be time to start to seriously think about starting or enlarging the herb section in your garden. Use a proper seed drill for this exercise and try to keep the plants about 20 centimetres or so apart to begin with because one never seems to know exactly how herbs will grow.

Start with some chives, chervil, sorrel, parsley and marjoram. Sow the seeds about 2–3 centimetres deep. How much you put out, relates entirely to your personal use – it depends on whether you want herbs for use at the table or to keep for storage.

Once the Moon has entered Libra, you plan out exactly when and where you should begin to plant out any new trees or bushes you may have obtained. This month is relatively ideal for planting out trees, bushes and, with the Moon in Libra, is just about the best time possible. Ornamental, apple, peach or cherry trees or bushes will flourish well if put in now.

In addition, this is also a good period for hedge extension and/ or their renewal. At some time during this month, you should have spent some time cleaning out your hedge(s) because they are always used by some kind of animal life, even if only for the temporary cover they provide. As a rule, a well-placed hedge is so useful as a windbreak, for it provides a useful shelter for all kinds of flowering shrubs and other plants as well.

On top of this, the benefits of having a colourful area here instead of just a plain old hedge, are rather obvious. Also, this month is really more or less the last time you can reasonably expect success from planting, adding to, or trimming a hedge. If you try to do any of this later in the year, any fresh root life may not have enough time to gain enough maturity or become as established as you might like.

As the Moon enters Scorpio, start to cut, graft and prune wherever you deem it is needed. Check greenhouse temperatures now because, while they ought to be reasonably even through the day, there is always the chance of a surprise frost somewhere.

While it is appreciated this area may well now be a tad cluttered with all your new seedlings and cuttings, all of which need light, but they also need protection from sudden temperature changes as well.

Always assuming the government haven't declared otherwise, the clocks should be put on one hour (spring forward) in the early hours of the last Sunday in March, for the official start of British summertime.

As the Moon journeys through Sagittarius, it is time to sow out main crop leeks again. A few early shallots won't hurt if started about now, and, of course, it never really hurts to put out onions and onion sets at this time either. Creating onion sets from onions is now not only popular, but quite acceptable in areas where onions themselves don't seem to do too well. So, quite a few gardeners actually put out their young sets now, planting them just below the surface. Try to use a trowel for this because the sets don't push themselves out too strongly.

Once the Moon enters Capricorn, ease back a little on actual gardening work to allow you time to attend to the condition of your tools and other equipment that you have been using, for this should have been one very busy month. Ensure that each item is well-cleaned. If you have the equipment and are able to do so, then bring everything into proper use, especially if edges need to be sharpened. Take care when dealing with any or all electrical machinery.

When the Moon moves into Aquarius, it is not too favourable a time for actual gardening. So much so that now is a good time to check up on weather damage that may have occurred. These days, we don't seem to have the fierce winds normally associated with this month but when it does blow this month, these winds can do a lot of damage that we may not appreciate until we go out into our garden the morning after the night before. Do make sure to check on the ties you put in place earlier to secure plants to stakes and wires. Also, make sure your labels, where you may have had to use them, are still in position.

If you can find the time, it won't hurt to start to pot on any rooted cuttings because quite a few flowers will be starting to show about now. However, if you feel they need it, then by all means keep them in a shaded place for a few more days. After this, you can put them into the sunlight. Similar work should also be carried out on your patio, if you have one. Re-pot plants where needed and ensure that any drainage arrangements are working well.

April

FOR AS LONG as the weather permits, clean up lawns, repair little lumps and bumps and mow – more than once, for you may feel it to be necessary. They can take it now that spring is finally here. Further, the more frequently you mow now, the less time you will have to spend gathering up and disposing of the clippings. Nevertheless, keep an eye open for little touches of frost because it doesn't take much to kill off young plants.

Having said that, this can be a pretty wet period and you may be limited in the amount of time that you can spend out in the open. So, in the event of too much wet weather, turn your attention to any indoor plants you may have. Now is the time to give them a thorough dusting and remove any dead leaves.

If needs be change the soil where you think it might be helpful and, when you have completed all this, give them all a slight watering, but nothing too heavy. It won't hurt to divide, layer or take a few cuttings of any plants because they are well protected and they can take it.

Dependent on whether you have a patio and then, if it is a covered area or not, now is the time to prepare troughs and boxes for new growths and sow a few hardy annual seed in the smaller pots. If your patio is a wooden structure and in need of a paint job, April is an ideal time to start your renovation work. If your area is a stone or metal construction, use a spray to clear away some of the marks you simply haven't had the time to clean up before.

Those with raised beds rather than pots on their patio, should extend their care to these items as well. Also, please make sure that the elderly and infirm can manage to get about the area freely. A useful tip here is to put your containers on wheels to assist free movement when you need to clean up.

Should you still need to work under cover, transfer your attentions to the greenhouse, where you may have to spend quite a bit more time than originally expected. Ventilation must be looked at and the temperature level must be kept fairly even. This will be especially so, if you experience hot days and cold nights.

The wind is another problem, so be careful of leaving any side windows or doors open for too long. Also, you will now be aware that a few pests have arrived, mostly spiders and greenfly. When you do meet up with them, dispose of them as instructed on any canned pest destroyer you may have purchased.

Once outside, all of your vegetable areas will need some love and care, along with some extra plantings needed to keep up the supply. Although it will be the middle of June before you do anything properly, think where you want to put your celery and then prepare the necessary trenches.

These should be at least 80–90 centimetres apart and about half that for single rows. Dig down about 35 to 40 centimetres, break up the base and mix in manure and well decayed refuse, if you have any. Add a level of top soil and more manure, until you have a soft layer about 10 centimetres deep in which to place the young plants later.

We turn now to what you might want to call successional sowings of vegetables, to keep up a regular supply of all your garden goodies.

More carrots, broad beans, peas, lettuces, potatoes, radishes and mustard and cress will all be helpful.

If you have the room, plant out asparagus crowns, more broccoli and even early winter cabbage. Once you have planted all that you feel you can manage, you must remember to keep these areas free from weeds and pests.

Earth-up where needed and don't be afraid to use a hoe where you can't get in by hand. Thin out parsnips sown earlier so that they will have enough room to develop properly – allow about 20 centimetres apart within each row. If you have the time, you could set up your runner bean supports now. Initially, allow one seedling to a support, held by loose string. If you tie too tight now, the plant will be unable to expand or extend properly. You may use seedlings or sow direct as you think fit.

There is no reason why you cannot add to your herb garden this month. Plant out rooted cuttings of bay; sow some dill, fennel mint, hyssop rosemary and sage. Some extra parsley will not hurt either. Harden off under glass what you can manage from your last month's exercises in this field.

The flower garden will take up a fair amount of your time this month, so it won't hurt to take cuttings from your herbaceous borders to use later. Delphiniums, phlox and lupins will all benefit from this. Finish planting out gladioli and attend to as many half-hardy annuals as you can. It won't hurt to plant out sweet peas, clematis, sweet Williams and foxgloves. If you have any, you can now make up hanging baskets with whatever suitable plants you have available. Verbena, geraniums and trailing plants always look nice here.

In the fruit garden it is time to keep a watching brief on your flowering apple, pear, cherry and plum trees. Rather than spray them with anything now, allow honey bees to do their thing and pollinate to their hearts content. But if you do spot problems, then take the appropriate action accordingly. Your gooseberries and blackcurrants will certainly benefit with a spray. Where you can, remove as many flowers as possible from strawberry plants and, while you are at it, spare a couple of minutes to look over your raspberries.

The work listed here for April is not complete by any means and is meant as a guide rather than as something written in tablets set in stone. The astrological advice referred to here should be taken in the same vein. While you ought to do this or do that, according to the phase of the Moon and where she is at any one time, this too should be read as a general guide because quite often it simply isn't possible to get everything done as stated. In these following paragraphs if something isn't mentioned in either category, it does not mean you should not carry out such tasks.

ASTROLOGICAL TIMING

Throughout any April, the weather can be rather notorious, what with high winds and sometimes quite hefty showers. So, keep an eye and an ear open for the local forecasts and work as best you can around what might clearly be adverse periods for working outside. Those of you with greenhouses and/or garden sheds can at least organise your working hours to suit these differences in the weather possibilities.

Once again, please also remember to be on the lookout for those occasional periods when the Moon travels void-of-course. While the shorter void of course Moon times are, more often than not, reasonably harmless, it is when the Moon is this way for the longer times that you should prepare to avoid the more serious aspect of gardening, such as starting anything new or something quite radical.

As the Moon begins her journey through Aries, you should try to spend some of your time preparing celery trenches, although they really aren't needed until June. But much depends on where you are, your particular expertise, and the way you like to work. However, the earlier you do this work, the more time there is for the manure and soil to become well blended in.

Use the space between the trenches for any future salad crops you might want to put in and, of course, as when the right time comes for such work.

Once the Moon begins to traverse Taurus, turn your attention to your lawns and other grassy areas. Spend as much time as you can and sweep up all these spaces with a stiff besom broom, remove worm casts and repair all those odd little patches and other bare spots you find. Mow your lawn and the other grassy bits first and then set to with your fresh grass seed. Rake the patch then scatter seed as evenly as you can and cover it with a small amount of reasonably dry soil. Cover these little areas with dark thread or little bits of netting to protect it all from bird damage.

When the Moon is in Gemini, the first of the Air signs, it is not too helpful because it does not favour planting or sowing. This is best for destroying any unwanted growths and weeds. Don't forget the damage that garden pests can do either. Keep an eye open for the damage they can create and get rid of them as well. In essence, it is time for a good clean up.

When the Moon passes on into Cancer, you may begin to pot out cyclamen seedlings that should be ready, sow zinnias in a frame. In the vegetable areas one may now plant both early and late potatoes, carrots and salsify, along with a few winter greens, some globe artichokes and asparagus. Also, you may put out a few runner beans, endive and parsley.

If you have the time, turn to the fruit section to put a protective spray on your gooseberries and black currants and don't forget to have a good look at your apples and pears, while you have a spray with you. And remember, if the Moon is in her first quarter, you should use a chemical base fertiliser on your roses. If the Moon is in Cancer, in her third or fourth quarters, it is more advisable to use an organic fertiliser.

Not a lot can be safely worked on when the Moon is in Leo, as a rule. Ideally, this is a good time to mow lawns to help ease their growth. Some vegetables and fruit may be collected in, if anything is ready. This is also a useful time for surveying and, perhaps, improving the look and uses of your patio.

If your patio is a wooden structure and in need of a paint job, April is an ideal time to start your renovation work. If your area is a stone or metal construction, use a spray to clear away some of the marks you simply haven't had the time to clean up before.

Those of you who have raised beds rather than pots on their patio, should extend their care to these items as well. Also, please make sure that the elderly and infirm can manage to get about the area freely. A useful tip, if you are planning for this idea where you are, it doesn't hurt to put your containers on wheels to assist free movement when you need to clean up.

You might want to create a few hanging baskets here and there to hang out later. Trailing plants always look nice in these carriers and geraniums seem to be at home here, along with verbena as well. Later on, you could add a few early "Busy-Lizzies" because when they do flower, they provide oodles of lovely colour.

However, once the Moon has pushed on into Virgo, you may relax a little and while you survey the month's work, do touch up here and there especially where you may have forgotten a task or two. The Moon here helps to produce flowers noted for their abundant growths, if started around now, or otherwise hoe, prepare that part of any of your patches you intend to use later.

Once the Moon has entered Libra, put out fresh alpines, plant herbaceous perennials and evergreen shrubs. Check greenhouse temperatures and keep them down from what they were through the winter period. On sunny days, open up top ventilation areas but leave the doors open only if there is little or no wind.

You may spray to prevent mildew forming on gooseberries and on pears, for they may well be due to flower shortly. Plum, cherry and apple trees need not be sprayed just yet because the bees ought to be out by now and they will be pollinating as if there were no tomorrow, if the weather is fine.

However, you may have to spray blackcurrants and you should find the time to remove as many flowers as you can from strawberry and raspberry plants. When the Moon enters Scorpio, it will be safe to take cuttings from lupins, delphiniums and phlox.

Dependent on whether you have a patio, and then if it is a covered area or not, now is the time to prepare troughs and boxes for new growths and sow a few hardy annual seeds in the smaller pots.

It could be about now that you might want to keep a few flowers in the house. Strictly speaking, there aren't any house plants as such but whatever you do have should be planted in when the Moon is in Taurus, Cancer, Libra, Scorpio or Pisces – depending on the month of course.

You may decide you do not want any plants inside the house at all, but do keep at least one pot of Aloe Vera because it is a most helpful healing plant, should you be burned, endure a minor cut or suffer an insect bite that really does sting.

Once the Moon has passed into Sagittarius it would be most helpful to get up your ladder to clean out guttering, drains and all the down pipes. With a little bit of thought, you will save yourself a lot of time later on in the year, creating little drain-hole covers – anything to stop the leaves and other debris from blocking them.

Once the Moon passes into Capricorn, plant or sow vegetables associated with the astrological signs of Taurus, Virgo and Capricorn. Swede, beetroot, carrots, potatoes and radishes all flourish if put in now. Put fresh straw around your strawberry plants and dust wherever you think you might suffer flea beetle attacks.

Once the Moon has moved into Aquarius, you should start to arrange supports for your runner beans. At first, one seedling per support is about the wisest move. Make sure they are tied well but not too tightly, otherwise the plant won't survive.

A Pisces Moon in April doesn't really support much in the way of fresh sowing or planting but you can use the time to work indoors. Give all your indoor plants a good dusting and take off all dead leaves and or petals. Some, if not all, could probably do with a complete change of soil if you have the time.

May

BY NOW IT is reasonably well into late spring or early summer, depending on your personal outlook, but you must still be on the alert for a few night frosts which can and do often occur out of the blue, despite any (official or unofficial) weather forecasts.

The best advice is to keep a few covers of whatever material you may have spare, even old newspapers will do the trick in most cases – just a precaution, you never know with this month. Just a simple frost can do so much damage at this time of the year.

Initially, and this may seem unreasonable, but do examine any or all new plants you buy or obtain from wherever, and that includes nursery or shop bought sources. It is a wise gardener who will empty out his (or her) new plants from their containers, shake the plant well and then re-pot with their own fine, fresh new soil. When a plant is bought in this manner it is always possible that you may also have bought in a few small white grubs which thrive on fresh young roots. This action determines they will get no further and you won't have to resort to spraying chemicals unnecessarily at a later date.

As the month progresses and it begins to warm, up watering well becomes a necessary daily task; perhaps twice a day in some areas. Hanging baskets suffer the most, as a rule, because they will almost certainly be hung in an exposed spot, bearing the brunt of the wind and sun.

Where possible, try to use rain water from your barrels. Most plants don't like too much tap water but if that is all you have then be gentle as you spray. Try to spray the roots of a plant rather than the plant itself.

As you carry out these little tasks, remember to water the roots of newly purchased shrubs and trees. It only takes a few dry days with a little bit of wind and the soil simply dries up. It does help if you mulch in a little manure or compost around the base, for this helps retain water. However, water first and then spread whatever you want to use afterward. Try to water in the early hours, not too late in the evening and certainly not during the middle of the day.

This is the right time of the year to run your eyes over any ponds you may have in your garden, whether they have fish in them or not. Duckweed and blanket weed will be heavy and you need to clear as much of this as you can. To offset this kind of growth, have a few floating water lilies on the surface, for when they begin to open their leaves, later on in the year, they will help to ease the problem.

Before you feed your fish, if you have any, that is, drain the pond as much as you dare without harming them, then refill it slowly until you have reached the desired levels. Although these creatures can and do tend to look after themselves, try to feed them at least every other day, but a little more often if they are active.

In among the flower beds now you should be prepared for signs of greenfly, especially on your rose plants. This may entail the use of a spray where there is a serious infection. It doesn't hurt to check out plum trees for the same problem, as greenfly tend to gather on these, although they seem to prefer the younger or newer growths.

Slugs are another more serious problem, for they love more or less all your younger plant life and they are terribly destructive creatures. Salt will be effective but is messy, so use either proprietary powders or slug pellets.

Incidentally, where there are slugs, there are often snails and they can be just as troublesome. If you pick them off plants by hand you can always leave them out in the open on a path – the birds will be down like a shot – especially parents with their young still in the nest.

If you thought you might have been busy in April, then May will certainly be a challenge as you move through the rest of your other flower beds. There is so much to attend to. You should now be planting out seeds of hardy and half-hardy annuals. Pot on carnations, plant out chrysanthemums, dahlias and, if you have any, other water plants. If you haven't already done so, you should now lift daffodil and tulip bulbs to create more space for your summer bedding plants.

Put down suitable catching material alongside your hedges and clip them where needed. Remove the clipping in the material and hold on to it. After this, hoe and weed as thoroughly as you can under the hedges. If you still have any heather left to plant out, mulch the ground first with peat and some of the hedge clippings and top dress the older plants. If you have any problems with your alpines, now is the time to weed with your hands or with a short hand held hoe, if you have one.

It is time now to turn to the vegetable plots for there is a lot of preparation work to be carried out this month. You will need to create the areas you want to use for marrows so that you may sow the seeds but thin them out later. Prepare a site for more tomatoes and also for cucumbers and courgettes under cloches. Sow some more summer spinach, main crop peas, endive and kohlrabi if you wish.

You will also want to sow more lettuce, radishes, mustard and cress. It won't hurt to put in a few more turnip seeds either and, perhaps, some chicory and chard seeds would be helpful now. Also this month, you may now plant out winter greens from earlier sowings, some celery and tomatoes.

Quite a few vegetable and flower plants can now be safely taken from the greenhouse or from under other sheltered places. This means you will have more room to start other exercises, perhaps not this month but at least you could have a good clean-up now that you have the space. Check under the greenhouse for small animal life and, while you are at it, check under the garden shed. You will be surprised at what you might find. Mice love this space and don't be surprised if you find a rat hole either. Take the necessary action quickly.

Fruit bushes will have to be looked at during this month so, when you have time, remember to prune your raspberries, remove extra or unnecessary runners from strawberries and spread some straw under them to protect the fruit as it matures.

Once again, please remember that the tasks for this month, referred to here, are not a complete list by any means. It simply isn't possible to get everything done as might be hoped, for there is so much to do and you may not have the time to get it all done. Also, the astrological advice that follows on now should be taken in much the same way. Keep to the days and times because that is important, but it may not always be possible to carry out all these tasks where your personal time is concerned.

ASTROLOGICAL TIMING

There is a very old saying (the actual words do bear slight change from area to area) that goes:

"Ne'er cast a clout until May is out."

Most folk take this as meaning that one should not leave off too much warm clothing until June arrives while others mean until the (May-bush) hawthorn bush produces flowers. So, as there is still the possibility of a frost, even this late into the year it would be a wise move to keep a few old cloths, papers, broken up cardboard boxes, and so on, ready – just in case.

Clever gardeners not only thoroughly check their new plant purchases, they also make a point of emptying new growths of the soil in which they came and re-pot them with fresh foil.

New purchases are liable to have unwanted animal life that will eat young plant life roots. If you make a point of cleaning off the old soil now it will remove this problem so that you shouldn't have to spray unnecessarily later.

Once the Moon passes into Aries ease up on any planting activities in favour of a thorough clean up everywhere. As usual, clean your gutters and down pipes, weed the edges of lawns as well as all other grassy areas. Make sure drains have been cleared through and sweep paths and drives. Once again, give your hedges a reasonably light beating and remove all the waste material that will drop out.

Once the Moon starts her journey through Taurus, complete any odd jobs that may still be outstanding. Now you can begin to plant and sow pretty much what you want, for this is a most fruitful Earth sign. Flowers noted for their hardiness should be planted out now and by all means feel free to fertilise as and where you wish, for the sign encourages the exercise.

Hanging baskets often suffer from a lack of regular watering, most probably because they are hung in exposed places which attract the wind and sun. It would be rather useful to use rain water from your barrels if you have any because most plants prefer it to tap water. You may also create a few completely new window boxes or hanging baskets during this lunar spell.

When the Moon starts her travels through Gemini, you might well find signs of greenfly, especially on the roses. Use a spray where they are in serious profusion and, while you are doing this, it won't hurt to look at plum trees, for greenfly can also have a field day here.

Yet another couple of pests are slugs and snails which are such destructive characters. For the slugs you can use salt, which is effective enough but awfully messy – it is far better to use the proprietary materials. Snails can be picked off wherever you find them and left out in the open on a path – the birds will be down like a shot.

Once the Moon has entered Cancer, it will be a good time to cast your eyes over your pools and ponds, whether there are fish in them or not. Blanket weed and duckweed are always heavy at this time of the year and must be cleared away. A few floating water lilies may well help keep them down a little but you will still have to take action yourself.

Prior to feeding fish, drain as much of the water out as you can without harming them. You must always refill slowly until the pond returns to its normal level. This is best achieved by laying the hose around the top with the end slightly over but with the water running fairly slowly. Although fish can and do look after themselves quite well, try to make a point of feeding them every other day but, perhaps, a little more often when they are active.

With the Moon in Leo, a rather barren sign that really doesn't favour sowing or planting at all, use what time you have to clean all your electrical tools carefully – and this does mean checking the wiring, plugs and fuses. By doing this work now, you will save yourself a lot of time but it doesn't hurt to do it relatively regularly – just think how often you reach for a tool without appreciating this aspect of its care. If you have the time, now is also a good time to look over other cutting equipment and clean and re-sharpen where needed.

The Moon will now pass into Virgo, a fruitful Earth sign in some ways. Flowers noted for their abundant growing talents do well. Using a chemical killer is also favoured at this time.

Hoe between the rows of onions, thin beetroot and carrot seedlings and, if you have, the time prepare fresh ground for planting out tomatoes in the greenhouse.

With the Moon in Libra, sow cucumbers and marrows outdoors. It is preferable to sow them singly (some gardeners plant them in pairs) and keep them about 25–30 centimetres apart, cover them with around 2–3 centimetres of soil and then place upside down flower pots to protect them from any enquiring small animal life. Any plant with a root growth should flourish well, if put out now

When the Moon travels through Scorpio, for good results, you should plant out flowers that are attractive and have strong fragrances; plant seeds of half-hardy and hardy annuals, work with chrysanthemums, dahlias and carnations. Sow marrows, courgettes and plant any previously sown leeks you put in earlier this year.

This sign also encourages grafting and pruning activities as well and, as the Moon is in Capricorn, also helps recovery from being cut. About any exercise of this nature started now may also be safely carried over the short period while the Moon is in Sagittarius as well.

This is also an almost perfect time to mulch around fruit trees. Spread a reasonable amount of well-rotted farmyard or stable manure around all type of fruit trees and bushes. With the Moon at the height of her powers in this cycle, as well as being in an Air sign, this will help feed the plants with much needed nourishment and will also help keep moisture flowing.

The Moon in Sagittarius encourages shallot seeds, although it is largely a barren sign. Some authorities recommend reaping fruit and vegetables at this time but experience suggests that this is not a good idea at all.

Once the Moon has passed into Capricorn, make sure you carry your pruning equipment with you as you work through your tree and bush areas. Your raspberries will almost certainly need some attention, as will your strawberries.

Plant out winter greens, sow dwarf French beans, beetroot, chicory and plant out more tomatoes. If you sowed any celery last month, it will need to be pricked out about now and if you have any leeks, they ought to be blanched. This may be accomplished with small stiff paper tubes about 15–20 centimetres by about 8–10 centimetres wide slipped over the tops of the plant, tied gently and earthed up a little.

When the Moon moves through Pisces, sow more lettuce, mustard and cress, radish, some turnip seeds and chard. The Moon here almost always seems to stimulate growth. In which case, if you want to experiment, this is always a good time to try anything reasonable out.

June

AS THIS MONTH opens many people take it for granted that, unofficially at least, summer begins on the 1st of June each year. While that may be true, it is still going to be a busy period. In normal circumstances, a gardener would have a few priorities, in that this takes precedence over that, or that this must be done before now and so on.

June is slightly different. Much of the gardener's time should be spent among the flower beds rather more than usual. Fruit trees and bushes will be high on the list while the vegetable food sections, although busy as usual, will need a trifle less attention.

Hardy herbaceous borders will need to be cut back and much work will have to be spent on the various types of roses you have. Cut away any small side shoots, hoe well between the plants and water well miniature roses. Hybrid and tea roses will shortly be coming into their own and making their rather striking appearance this month.

Train the climbing and the rambler roses thoroughly, otherwise they will go mad and simply overtake their part of the garden, to the detriment of neighbouring growths. Remove all sucker shoots where you see them. Elsewhere, deadhead all other roses, either if they have faded or, of course, are serving no more useful purpose. This can be done by hand most of the time, otherwise use secateurs. This will allow the plant to conserve its energies into producing only the best.

Established lawns will need to be mowed regularly. If the weather is dry then spike the lawn first. Clean away all weeds, apply new seed and cover with a little piece of netting to keep the birds away. Lift as many remaining spring bulbs as you can and prepare them for storage. It won't hurt to lightly trim hedges because they may need it. However, when you have finished, gather in the trimmings to keep for mulching. Hoe and weed as well as you can under all plants.

Usually, this can be a fairly dry period, so it wouldn't hurt to clear all your plants out of the greenhouse to allow you back in with a hose and cleaners. It isn't a pleasant task but it does have to be done and you'll be surprised at just what has gathered that had not caught your eye before. Remember to allow for night time ventilation which will mean keeping an eye on the local weather forecast.

Pools and water plants should be looked at because if the weather is sultry or a tad too warm, there will be signs of aphids and midges. Algae often grows a lot more about now and that will need to be removed. Lower the water level and replace gently with fresh water from a hose or a spray if fish are present.

Alpines and heathers shouldn't need a lot attention but they will have to be weeded in the usual way. Clip where the plant is obviously untidy or would benefit in a similar way to the way you worked your roses earlier. Heathers like a gentle spray when you water them and it is wiser to do this in the early evening hours, where possible.

Many of you will have hanging baskets dotted about here and there and they will need a lot of attention in the dry weather. Hose the roots of these plants thoroughly and let the water really cover the surface of the soil. Pin back any over long trailers, to improve their general appearance.

We turn now to the vegetable garden and the work needed here. It will be much the same as last month, with certain exceptions. It is important to earth up all of your recently planted potatoes but not all at once.

Take it steady and start the work a little bit at a time. It would be helpful if you pursued this task on three or even four occasions, to give the plants a chance.

Sow lettuce, turnips, endive, a few more peas, radishes and mustard and cress. Plant out winter cabbage, sprouts, kale, savoy and greens. It wouldn't hurt to start some more celery about now, a little more chicory, certainly a few swedes, marrows, and, if you think you can do it well, why not try a few leeks? Later in the month, try your hand at some spinach beet using the method we described in April for beetroot.

Apart from mentioning an odd job here and there, fruit hasn't exactly been at the top of the list. This month it will quite be the reverse, for there is so much to get done. All fruit trees and bushes must be carefully checked over for any infestation and if any is found, it must be dealt with promptly and with the right materials.

All fruit is prone to something during June, and strawberries are no exception. Look for grey mould and damage by birds, slugs and all pests in between. Limit runners to what you feel you can reasonably handle. Strawberries, along with gooseberries, may be thinned out or harvested accordingly. As a rule, I can usually selectively pick raspberries in the first week of June.

Apples and pears will need to be thinned out, as will peaches and nectarines. Cherries, plums, damsons and currants will need to be thinned, watered well and, if necessary, added protection may be made by applying threads of ordinary cotton spread among the branches, because it will stop the birds from invading the plants.

For those who decided to entertain herbs this year, sow fresh dill, some chervil and put in a few cuttings of sage and rosemary. Pickings will be rich now, so you can start to gather in either for more or less immediate use or for freezing.

The leaves of rosemary, mint and sage may be gathered in as can sorrel, parsley, mint and fennel. Individual instructions for how each herb should be prepared for freezing ought to be found on the original packets that they came in.

In town gardens or on patios, it is important that you water regularly – at least once a day if you can. If this is not possible, it would be a good idea to top dress the plants with a little damp peat. Remove dead flower heads and, if needs be, you can always replace these growths with some of those from the garden.

The work listed here for June is not everything that could or should be done, but has been created more as a guide than anything else. In the following paragraphs you are given guidance as to when you should carry out these tasks in line with the phase and position of the Moon, but even this is not complete either. Because it isn't mentioned in either category, does not mean you should not attempt the tasks.

ASTROLOGICAL TIMING

This is about the time the gardener who has no astrological knowledge should be advised of what the void-of-course moon means. Some of the periods only last for a few minutes or even hours and, as such, the event should be taken as reasonably harmless. It is when the moon becomes void–of-course for any longer time, then you should try to avoid the more serious aspect of starting anything new or something quite radical.

In June, and when the Moon starts to travel through Aries, find the time to have a good clean up everywhere. Pick up all those bits and pieces that you have rather studiously ignored for some time. Get a good tough garden bag and pack away all those bits and pieces of twig, dead plants, wrappers and whatever else doesn't quite fit in to the garden anywhere.

Mow all the grassy areas, sweep all the paths and drives. The difference will surprise most of you more than you might think.

As the Moon moves into Taurus, you will probably find yourself spending quite a bit of time in the flower beds rather more than usual. The fruit sections will need attention but that can come later. If you have herbs, sow fresh dill, some chervil and put in a few cuttings of sage and rosemary. Pickings will be rich now so you can start to gather in mint, rosemary, sage, parsley and fennel, all for more or less immediate use or for freezing.

It would be helpful to remove any loose runners from both strawberries and violets now because they can be quite prolific if left alone.

Once the Moon pushes on into Gemini, it may well be during a fairly dry spell. If this is so, completely clear all the plant life out of your greenhouse, then go back in with your hose and your cleaning bits and pieces – and don't forget the oil for all the hinges.

No matter how often you get around to this, you will almost always be surprised at what has accumulated since you did it all the last time. Remember to allow for night time ventilation, once you start to put things back, and be ready to drop the top ventilator because the night time temperatures in June can be a lot colder than you may have originally allowed. Once all these little jobs have been finalised, gently water well everywhere.

The Moon in Cancer suggests a quick look at your heather and alpine plants. Weed as you might normally do and clip where the plant or plants seem untidy. An easy gentle spray will help finish this job.

It matters very little where your hanging baskets may be but they always seem to need a lot of attention especially about now. The plant life in these arrangements must be thoroughly watered on a regular basis and, for once, it doesn't hurt if you actually cover the surface soil with water. Trim or pin back any overly long trailers coming out of the containers.

Once the Moon is established in Virgo, turn your attention to your fruit bearing plants. If you haven't done so already, you must check them out for infestation of any kind and, where found, it must be dealt with properly and promptly.

During June so much can happen and, for a start, the strawberries will be no exception. Damage from local bird life, grey mould, slugs and other pests could be worse than you first think. Thin out gooseberries and strawberries or pick them, of course. Raspberries ought to be ready by now as well.

Look at your other fruit as well. There is so much to cover here but, of course, that all depends on what you may have in your garden. Thin out and clean away pest damage on damsons, cherries, apples, pears, peaches, plums, nectarines and all currant varieties as well. If you think it is needed, spread ordinary cotton between the tree and bush branches, for that will deter the birds from getting in and destroying the fruit.

With the Moon in Scorpio, now is the time to move into the vegetable areas for work will be needed here. Earth up all of recently planted potatoes and check out the status of other root vegetables.

Once this has all been dealt with, spend as much time as you can variously sowing mustard and cress, lettuce, radishes, turnips, endive and more peas. You may also plant out savoy and winter cabbage, sprouts, greens and kale.

Celery can be started and more chicory won't go amiss. If you have the space, try a few leeks, marrows and swedes. If you haven't already tried to do so, put in some spinach beet using the method described for beetroot.

The Moon in Sagittarius encourages odd jobs that a lot of people either will not take for granted or they won't get involved in at all. Simply pottering around as you see fit will cause you to make a mental note of many little tasks that should have been completed by now. For example, you could see to the lawn and grassy areas in this period because just about all grassy areas will need regular attention and mowing at this time of the year. Should the weather be dry, it would be a good idea to spike the lawn first.

If you have collected any weeds in the lawn, now is the time to mend – not just make do. Clear away the weeds and their roots as far as you can, put in new seed and cover the new patches with pieces of netting to keep the birds away. Once again, it never hurts to trim hedges but at this time of the year, when you do this, keep the trimmings for mulching. Hoe and weed as well as you can between and under all plants.

Once the Moon starts her journey through Capricorn, cut back on your herbaceous borders. Work on your roses. Remove side shoots, hoe between them and water your miniature roses. As tea and hybrid roses are about to come into their own, many may need to be disbudded., Take off as many of the buds as you can, for this will allow what you have left to flourish more easily.

Rambler and climbing roses will need to be well trained, so cut them back or they will just take over the area. Cut off the sucker shoots, deadhead other roses whether they have faded or are serving little purpose now. It is important to use a good pair of secateurs for this work.

The Moon in Aquarius allows a certain amount of leeway when it comes to pursuing an experiment or just following the normal rules of gardening while she travels through this rather barren Air sign. The usual clean-up activities apply, but this is also rather a good time to harvest and store some of the fruit as it comes to picking time.

Once the Moon begins her journey through Pisces, it is time to look at all your pond areas. If the temperature is high and it has been dry for a while, empty out about two thirds of the water, cleaning away any of the dregs and algae as you go. Refill slowly and gently with your hose, especially if you have fish. The best way to do this is lay the hose around the top of the pond and let it refill slowly to maintain temperature and not stir up too much dross.

In the event of any excessive growth of aquatic plant life while involved in this exercise, lift it out and divide it. The longer the plant life has been there, the better. The water will appear to look a tad murky while you carry out this task but that is to be expected. It all settles back but may take a day or two to really get back to normal.

July

HOPEFULLY, THIS WILL be the best month of the year with those long hazy days of summer where we can all lounge out and enjoy the fruits of our labours – in more ways than one perhaps. Unfortunately, it doesn't always work that way because extreme weather conditions frequently happen in July. A look back over previous years has shown that in the last week, there are often terrible rain storms that simply seem to appear from nowhere.

Astrologers are well aware that rain can be quite heavy when the Moon is in any of the Water signs, especially Scorpio but, curiously, even more so when she passes through the Earth signs. By now, most of you will have picked up this knowledge for yourselves. All you have to now is keep a weather (?) eye open and be prepared. It doesn't happen every year but, when it does, it can leave even the most disbelieving of people gasping.

You will be busy in the flower beds and among your fruit trees, bushes and other plants. All flowers will need your attention. Lilies will need to be dead headed but do remember to keep them to extract their seeds. Dig up and divide irises, trim chrysanthemums and ensure young dahlia plants are well tied up. Roses should be cut for their display and alpines will need to be continuously weeded and trimmed, as will all hedges and other bush growths.

Water loss in your ponds is always a threat because of the heat so as you renew always do it slowly and gently. Lay the hose into the water and let the water run in slowly – the fish will prefer that. While you carry out this work you will probably have to thin out quite a few pond plants because they will be threatening other life as they mature and multiply. Do this by lifting the plant to the side but not out of the pond. This not only allows the plant to dry but also for any pond life to get back where it belongs.

Most gardeners tend to have watering of all kinds for the visiting wildlife. Do make sure bird baths and their drinking places are kept full and fresh, while also doing the same for landlocked creatures who come either by day, like the squirrels, or at night, like the foxes and, in special areas, the badgers. You may never know or see your guests at night but they do pass through. Sometimes they are most brazen while at others you would never know what they get up to.

In the greenhouse, many plants would do better to be in frames, pots or whatever, rather than out in the open in there. The overly careful gardener may well have young grapes growing in their greenhouse and, if so, they will need very careful attention and thinning about now. The same goes for any heavy crop tomatoes that are grown in here. Ensure everything in the greenhouse is kept well watered but do it gently.

In your vegetable patches, you will be more inclined to harvest what you have already put out, one way or another, but to keep up the momentum, more will have to follow to ensure you have plenty. During July you will need to water everywhere most thoroughly but, as elsewhere in your garden this must be done in a more leisurely fashion, for you can do a lot of damage with too much direct or hard watering with a hose that is locked on full.

As fast as you gather in artichokes, potatoes, onions, shallots, salad plants, runner beans, herbs and anything else you have chosen to be in your particular garden, you will also have to plan out where your fresh vegetables will be planted or sown. Leeks should be put out this month, as should spinach, beet, swedes, turnips, winter cabbage and broccoli. The larger type of radish may be sown out with a few more peas, potatoes, carrots and cauliflower, to name but a few.

Find the time to spend in your herb garden that you have been developing. When you gather in your herbs it is important to keep them apart – very few mix with other varieties. Pick only what you need. It won't hurt to plant out more chervil, dill and parsley in open ground. Don't forget that lavender is counted as an herb and should be treated accordingly. Fruit of all kinds should be harvested this month – apples, pears, cherries, gooseberries, currant and whatever else you personally have cultivated.

After picking, you need to thin or prune your trees and bushes, which is an almost thankless task at this time of the year because there is so much to think of as well as keeping a normal eye on their overall healthy appearance. The slightest appearance of any infestation, bugs or similar, must be dealt with efficiently and immediately or the rest could suffer.

If you have the time, and because you will almost certainly appreciate a mushroom, for they have a most unique taste, but you may find your present yield may not be quite up to expectation, you might have to look at preparing a new mushroom bed. These edible fungi don't require too much attention, but creating a first-time patch does need a little effort and July is almost perfect for this exercise.

As usual, the tasks listed here for July are far from complete and have been compiled as a guide only. However, these astrologically based suggestions for when and what jobs with which you should try to time with the phase and position of the Moon are not complete either. Because it isn't mentioned in either category does not mean you should not carry out such tasks.

ASTROLOGICAL TIMING

Once the moon moves into Aries, and we start the whole run-around yet again, it will be important to make the effort to clean and sharpen all garden and house tools, at least as far as you can. While you are doing these small tasks, this temporary breather from actual sowing and planting will give you the opportunity to examine everywhere for all the usual infestations that are liable to occur at this high point of the year.

It is best to remove (as far as possible, of course) all plum tree branches where silver leaf has attacked. To stop the spread of this organism, you have little choice but to cut away the branch and paint the new open end with a good preventative against the disease. It is also wise to spray apples against moth infection about now as well.

As the Moon approaches and passes into Taurus, sow some endive, cauliflower, broccoli and more parsley if you need it. At this time of the year, it won't hurt to add winter cabbage, celery and, if you need them, extra tomatoes. If you have the space, add a little more mustard and cress, lettuce, radishes and summer spinach.

Once the Moon passes into Gemini try to make the greenhouse your next priority and have a good clear out. You will probably have many plants that would be far better off in pots, frames or even boxes, in some cases.

Careful gardeners who cultivate grapes may well have a few that will need special attention about now. Thin them out carefully and, if you have any, do the same with any tomatoes growing in here. Once you have cleaned and tidied up again, with everything more or less in place again, water well everywhere but gently.

As the Moon pushes on into Cancer, it is time to take a good look over your herb garden. You should begin by gathering in what may be ready. Remember to keep all the herbs you harvest well apart from each other until you want to use them. Herbs tend not to mix that easily with other varieties. Put out more dill and chervil and work on a small lavender plot, not an easy plant to deal with at the best of times but so rewarding when it does take.

Fruit of all kinds now need to be picked – or many will, because this is the time when everything suddenly seems to ripen all at once. Gooseberries, currants, apples and pears, cherries and whatever else you have personally grown. Follow all the rules for their storage or for other usages, such as freezing.

And it won't stop there this month because, as the Moon enters Leo, it will be time to gather in onions, shallots and leeks, salad plants, artichokes, potatoes, runner beans and more or less anything else you personally wanted to grow.

When the Moon passes into Virgo you should take the opportunity to layer your border plants, especially carnations. This plant may well give a better result if you take the time be selective in your choice, because the non-flowering shoot often does much better when you replace some of the soil around it with potting soil, mixed with peat and sand. It won't hurt to put out more salad ingredients, to make the supply as regular as you can get it. Sea kale and spinach beet should also be put out while the Moon is in this sign.

However, as the Moon moves on into Libra and, if you lack sufficient time, you can still pursue these activities. In addition, you will have also to manage to work among other flower beds, around the fruit trees and bushes and other plants. All the flowers will have to be overseen, one way or another. Lilies should be dead headed, but keep the heads so that you may take out the seeds before you finally dispose of them altogether.

Now would also be a fine time to trim chrysanthemums, cut roses for in-house displays and then begin to summer prune them. Irises should be dug up and divided and don't forget to weed in among your alpines. After this, trim hedges and bushes where needed. Lawns mown now will help to slow down their growth quite a bit. If you are going to spread any fertiliser around now, an organic one will do the job twice as well as a chemical one, in this period of the Moon.

Once the Moon starts to occupy Scorpio, summer prune cherries and plums and thin out apples and pears where needed. Most bushes will need to be tidied up about now so prune all these growths. You may have already decided to take on a few grafting exercises in various places and the Moon in Scorpio is an ideal place for this activity. Although the Moon has to traverse Sagittarius first, by the time she passes into Capricorn, it will help the healing process beautifully.

While in Sagittarius the Moon is in a suitable place for you to check for vermin, pests and bugs wherever they decide to appear. This is especially so when you make a check for butterfly eggs on the underside of the leaf. Crush or kill them with a spray. By the time the cabbage is ready for the table, these leaves will either have been long gone or you will have cut them away during preparation.

Once she has started her journey through Capricorn, sow or plant out more turnips, parsnips, carrots, radishes and swedes. Curiously, a Full Moon in this sign is one of the best places and times to pick and eat mushrooms, although the Full Moon in any sign is equally as suitable.

Should your supply of fresh mushrooms be getting a tad short, now is an excellent time to create a new bed. Place any new bed by a north facing wall but under cover. You may make it as wide or as long as you wish, but for a really successful harvest, try to make it somewhere around 50 to 70 centimetres in depth.

When the Moon appears in Aquarius during July, she is giving you a chance for collecting, picking and harvesting anything and everything where you can. Lift and store autumn grown onions now. If you have the opportunity, take the smaller chrysanthemum flower buds, leaving the bigger ones to bloom as they will. Take the time to also clean through drains and pipes, remove debris then sweep up generally.

While on this general clean-up, it doesn't hurt to pay some attention to the tops of any walls you may have in or around the garden. There may be no plant life, as such, but there will almost certainly be some weeds and other things. A clean top here always gives that extra "bling" to any garden. Visitors always appreciate any place that looks as though it is being well looked after.

Once the Moon is in Pisces, make time to look over the condition of ponds and all the watering holes you may have prepared for all your visiting wildlife. The loss of water in a pond (probably because of the heat) is always a worry, so it won't hurt to drain it at least half way again and renew with fresh water, slowly and gently. Lay the hose on the edge of the pond and just let it run in until it is full again.

Please ensure that all bird baths, drinking places and other watering holes are kept full and fresh. Landlocked animals, like squirrels, foxes or even a hedgehog or two as well as badgers, will be grateful. You may never know or see your guests at night, but you when do have them pass by, you will feel better knowing they can get a drink as they do go. Sometimes you know they have been because of their actions, as they can be quite brazen, while at other times you would never know what they get up to.

The Moon in Pisces creates the time to allow you to pay attention to your strawberry beds, it is also the time for new beds to be well dug in, that is, if they are needed. You will need to apply plenty of manure and it won't hurt to throw in some bone meal for good measure. Flowers planted out now almost always flourish well if put in at this time.

You may well have to thin out some of your other plant life about now. However, before you cut or try to remove anything from around or near the pond areas, pull the selected growth(s) to the side. This is to allow for anything that has accidentally been caught up to free itself. Either that or, if you see any movement, you can assist as and when.

August

THIS A FUNNY old month because there is not really any set pattern to which you need seriously stick and yet there is so much to do. More importantly perhaps, this is often the best time for most folk to go on holiday, and then hope that whoever you asked to mow the lawn and water the rest of your garden, actually does so while you are away.

So, in August you need not only to keep picking away from your vegetable patches, harvesting in all your goodies, you must also plan out where you are going to sow or plant fresh or even completely new stock. As it is now high summer this is a good time to pick cabbage, marrow and courgettes. Pick beans as fast as you can and, if there are too many to eat within a few days or so, pick them for freezing.

As August rumbles on it is always a good time to lift onions as gently as you can from the soil, prepare and dry them. If you do this properly, they will stay reasonable for as long as you store them well. Beetroot will need to be harvested and, as you gather in cucumbers, check them over. If they show signs of not being as good as they have been in the past, it is time to get rid of all your early plantings and get ready to develop what you have growing in frames elsewhere.

Potatoes and tomatoes should still be giving a good yield at this time of the year, so feel free to pick and use as you see fit. Later in the month, you can always make a fresh planting or sowing, along with a fairly large array of other vegetables as well.

Fresh planting and sowing will now need to be carried out. More lettuce won't hurt, nor will seeds of spring cabbage and ordinary onions, for planting out in the early part of next year. You may also sow a few spring onions along with some Brussels sprouts. Winter spinach and spinach-beet may also be sown for winter use.

Early in the month, a few carrots may be sown in sheltered spots and a little more lettuce won't hurt, nor will a few more radishes. Mustard and cress will survive, as will endive. As long as these sowings are well protected, they should all serve you well as their time comes along. Should you decide to sow a little more tomato and cucumber, then for best results, you should keep them at a regular temperature preferably under glass.

In the fruit garden you will need to pick apples, pears, loganberries and what few grapes that ought to be ready, although it may be a tad early for these. Prune raspberries as they finish then turn your attention to pick off some of the late strawberries. Cherries and plums should be at their best by now, and a few early melons should be available about now.

All damaged fruit and vegetables should be thrown into the compost heap, as long as there is no evidence of pest damage. Where this is so, then throw them away or destroy them so that whatever the animal may be, it won't be able work its magic in the compost.

If a few strawberries are planted out about now, try not to keep them too close to each other. Place them at least 45 centimetres apart, as long as you have the space. Other stronger growing strawberry plants may be kept in pots and can be forced under glass for use next spring.

In among the flower beds there is much to maintain rather than start or pick anything, because the winds are liable to become a little stronger now, which can cause quite a few headaches. Growths of all kinds should be thinned carefully this month and plants that need to be tied should all have their ties checked thoroughly and adjusted, where necessary.

Plant or re-plant irises, cut gladiola for indoor display, attend to all roses for many will need to be removed as they fade, as the month wears on. Disbud dahlias, spray all flowers against infestation, especially in among the pinks and carnations. Remove the supports from any herbaceous border flowers that have finished flowering.

Lift the remaining flower bulbs that are left and prepare to plant out daffodil bulbs for next year. Also, colchicum, autumn flowering crocus and hardy cyclamen should be put out this month. The Madonna lily bulbs must be planted in August, unlike the other varieties of lily plants. Border carnations layered earlier can now be rooted out and planted where you want them. In the colder areas, it might be preferable to put them in pots.

Alpine plants should be sprayed, thinned and any cuttings you want, you should take now. In ponds and pools, the larger water lilies may need to have a few of their huge leaves cut away, to give the rest of the life in there a better chance. Trim hedges and always hoe and weed where you get in at their bases, for these growths should be maturing quite handsomely by now.

Lawns should be checked out, for many little patches begin to appear about now and must be renewed. Dig out the bad areas gently, apply a little compost, sow grass seeds, thumb them in firmly, then apply plenty of fertiliser about 10 days later. If rainfall seems to be fairly regular, no matter how heavy or light it may be, the lawn may not be watered as regularly or separately at this time of the year. When you mow, however, let the clippings stay on the lawn, for they will act as a mulch to help retain water.

As before, these tasks for the month ahead are not complete because it isn't possible to think of and get everything carried out properly. In August, there is much to do and if you holiday at this time then the work won't be finished as one might wish. The astrological advice given here must also be taken in much the same way. Where you can, keep to the days and times because, while it is important to do so, it isn't always that simple or easy either.

ASTROLOGICAL TIMING

While you should still observe the position and phase of the Moon as in other months, for most people August is the peak holiday period, whether you go away or not. Therefore, much of what you might normally do could have to be put on hold. Most of us have good neighbours who would be prepared to water the garden and, if need be, mow the lawn(s) but there is always the chance that he or she might not have been able to pursue anything while you were or away.

With this in mind please remember that the following suggestions to do this or that for when the Moon is here, there or wherever this month are only guidelines, if you are left up in the air for any reason.

So, during August, do what you have to do, as and when you can. Try to observe the astrological guidelines where you can but, as this is the peak of the year when everybody wants to be somewhere else, you can only do so much. Where possible, pick away in your vegetable patches, reaping in what needs to be gathered. It shouldn't be too difficult so, while you are at it try, to plan out where you are going to sow fresh or even completely new stock for the new year.

As this is the peak of summer, it would be best to bring in courgettes, marrow and cabbage. Check your beans on a daily basis and pick them as fast as you can. If you harvest a fair amount and cannot eat them all in a few days or so, then pick them and freeze them.

The Moon in Aries encourages the use of a bonfire, so that you are able to dispose of all the waste you want – but keep the ashes for use later on in the month. This is always a good month to have a clean through the guttering system because, if there are any signs of weakness, you have plenty of time to remedy the problem(s) yourself or call in the professionals., It won't hurt to run the hose through all the down pipes while you are at it.

At the end of August, a few leaves may well start to fall and the last thing you want is to have to spend any time unclogging pipes or whatever. So, if you can't do anything while the Moon is in Aries, then try to get the job done when she passes through Gemini or Aquarius.

Once the Moon is into Taurus, make sure you give the lawn and any of your other grassy patches a good mowing, but this month allow the clippings to lay there, for they will help retain moisture. It would also be useful to make a few successional sowings of vegetables about now. Sow or plant out carrots, radishes, mustard and cress, endive and lettuce. Seeds of tomatoes and cucumbers can be sown about now but, even at this time of the year, they will need to be kept at a fairly constant warm temperature.

The Moon begins her journey through Gemini, and this will be a good time to lift early beetroot. Cut back pansies and violets to ensure you will have a few little cuttings to use in September. Collect some of the old cyclamen corms, shake off the soil, trim down the old foliage and then re-pot into containers of an adequate size with a little compost, to get them started off well.

When the Water sign of Cancer receives the Moon, ensure that you sow winter spinach, and spinach beet. Earth up celery, sow spring cabbage and cabbage for pickling. Take cuttings from alpines, trim hedges and hoe and weed well underneath. Make sure the area is clear and clean and there are good gaps between it (or them) and any other plants near them.

There will almost certainly be an excess of growths of all kinds along the tops of ponds. Pull large plants to the edge and leave them there for a little while, in case there is any life caught up in them. Trim back everywhere else, refresh the water if you think it is needed and then remove the growths drying off on the side.

As the Moon passes through Leo, it won't hurt to keep doing what you have been doing but, where possible, turn the soil in any of the now empty vegetable patches and spread a little manure and any other mixtures you favour, to help plant growth. Where your raspberries have finished fruiting, it won't hurt to cut out the really old canes that fruited at or near the ground level. Keep a few back by all means, but the more you keep, the more you risk potential disease.

As the Moon begins to travel through Virgo, it signals that it is now time to put out your autumn flowering crocuses, daffodils and cyclamen. Root out carnations that you should have layered earlier, and plant another batch of Madonna lily bulbs, for this will be just about the last chance to do so this year – that is, if you want to ensure success.

After the Moon enters Libra, make a point of checking over your strawberry bed preparations and, where you feel it necessary to do so, adjust accordingly. Put in some winter lettuce, pot on winter-flowering begonias, sow stocks and, if you have the room, sow a small green crop area in vacant ground, if you have any.

As the Moon passes through Scorpio, and because runner beans and celery need a lot more moisture than usual, make sure you water them freely if the weather has not broken by now. Both tomatoes and potatoes will be flourishing well and giving good yields. Pick and use them as you see fit.

When the Moon enters Sagittarius, it implies that now is the time to completely clear out all waste green matter, all other unwanted growth and put them in the compost. Add a little sulphate of ammonia or just ordinary water and then turn it all over as thoroughly as you can.

This will help it rot down fairly evenly. Onions, shallots and leeks may all be put out and, if those already sown look as though they are ripening well, you can help out by lifting them a little to speed this up.

When the Moon starts to journey through Capricorn, have a good scout around your herb section. Gather in herbs you might want to use more or less straightaway or for freezing. You may also put out chervil, lamb's lettuce, landcress and winter purslane. These last three items make excellent substitutes in salads at any time or, indeed, in soups during the winter.

If you haven't already done so in your herb garden put out some teasel, poppy and lemongrass, for each of these herbs may be used for cooking or in meals. Lemongrass may also be used to make a bath quite an aromatic affair.

When the Moon is in Aquarius, whatever damaged fruit you find while wending your way around your fruit bushes and trees, picking off and collecting fallen damaged fruit and/or other growths, don't put them into the composter. It is better to destroy them, so that whatever has caused the trouble cannot (eventually) be spread elsewhere, when the time comes to use anything from this heap. If you are going to have a bonfire, then this is an even better way of getting rid of them. If neither of these options are possible, then bag it all up and put it in the (garden) rubbish bin.

As soon as the Moon passes into Pisces, you will find that any mushrooms picked about now will taste that little bit better. The nearer to any Full Moon you do this, the better they will be. While you are rummaging around here, make a point of doing a thorough check of the entire bed, to see if all is as it should be. If you are not satisfied, make any changes that you feel are necessary.

With the Moon well established in Pisces, make the time to work as diligently as you can through the flower section. Deadhead roses, disbud dahlias, replant gladioli and irises, and remove any runners from the violets. Check over any or all ties, to make sure they are firmly in place or have not been caught up in the bark anywhere. Spray pinks and carnations.

September

AUTUMN HAS ARRIVED and with it an occasional sample of much cooler nights but still with a few rather nice summer daytime periods. It is time to clear away the remains of any plant life that has now finished for the year. Cuttings should be taken from shrubs and selected flowers of your choice. Where possible, really clean through as much as possible, sweep the lawn, all the paths, the drive and the edges of the green areas where they lay against walls.

Before the really cold weather arrives, have all your garden (and home) electricity arrangements properly checked over by a professional, if you can't do it yourself. Cabling and weather-proofing involving these installations can start to lose their efficacy after the summer and, at the start of damp cold nights, the last thing anyone wants is a power failure at the first sign of a frosty spell.

Drains and gutters need to be totally cleaned through, so that all debris is moved out and you should run your hose through them to make sure you have cleared it all. If you have any need to work on major changes – anything from slightly re-designing the shape of your garden, to laying concrete, re-building or extending walls or the paving perhaps, then the early part of this month is the best time for such activities. Remember, concrete that has been affected by frost will simply fall apart once it has warmed up again.

When you clip your hedges, ensure you pull all weeds from the ground but don't just leave them lying on the ground, for they are liable to root again. Either destroy them in a small bonfire, along with any other rubbish you need to dispose of, or throw them on the compost heap. If you are planning any extra hedges, lengthening or strengthening present ones, then now is the time to get things ready, but not for planting just yet, because the ground should be left for several months.

Indoor plants should be moved away from window areas at night, but you may still allow them all the light they want during the day time. Indoor temperatures are usually fairly static, but even plants like to move with the times. Remove the faded or weakening plants, empty the pots and refill with fresh soil and a little manure. On outdoor patios, much the same should be carried out here as well. If you throw away old flowers, empty those containers too, but refill and prepare for planting spring bulbs. If you aren't going to use any of the containers, empty them and store until wanted again.

And while on the subject of light, September is an excellent month in which to create a new indoor mushroom bed. Although they may be grown almost anywhere, now is certainly a splendid period in which to create a new bed. For if started about now, mid-October will see your first pickings, which could last easily well into winter. Cover well with straw and keep lighting to a minimum, for mushrooms grow best in the dark.

Vegetables like spring cabbage may be planted out, and lettuce sown in a frame should help the winter supply somewhat. Prick out red cabbage, if you sowed any last month. Move parsley from the July sowing and transplant them, along with a few French beans, for forcing later.

Elsewhere, it is advisable to harvest other vegetables and certainly fruit should be gathered in now before frosts, if any, start to appear again. So, pick off apples and pears as they become ready, prune blackberries and peaches and tie the growths back well, to protect against possible high winds.

It is a good idea to have a thorough clean-up in among the fruit trees and bushes, clear away the deadwood, rake up the leaves and hoe, ready for new plantings of cane fruits like currants and gooseberries.

At this time of the year, because of the dampness about, mildew is a danger for all plants, although it should be possible for you to ease the problem by spraying with a good fungicide that has been created for this purpose. Alternatively, and especially indoors, a dry atmosphere may see an increase in red spider infestation.

Once again, use a spray, where you can, that has been created for this work as well. There are some people who swear by spreading cigarette, pipe and/or cigar ash over their webs. They claim this will also get rid of the little pests but, I would ask, where do they then go?

Much of the rest of the suggested work is, more or less, looking ahead. Early bulbs like scillas and pots of crocus are always welcome sights in the deep of winter, so now is a very good time to place corms or bulbs in their pots. Cuttings of bedding fuchsia and geraniums should be taken about this time of the year, for they will root readily in pots or a well-protected garden frame.

Plant out daffodil and narcissus bulbs now, for they will become quite strong and ready for your next year's showing. Along with these, you may also pot on or put in bowls all spring flowering bulbs. By all means, leave them in the garden for a few more weeks but, if it looks like being really frosty, bring them in or put them in the greenhouse.

You may have to begin to keep a watchful eye on your overnight heating arrangements in the green house now because the nights, if not frosty, will certainly be damp by the time morning arrives. Heavy dew is almost always expected as the month wears on, and you will see evidence of this when you move outside in the early hours.

And please try to remember to make sure any water and food containers for the visiting wildlife are kept clean and full.

All the tasks referred to here for September are fairly extensive but, as before, they cannot cover all that has to be done. The astrological advice however, while pertinent and to the point, may also be a tad limited. So in the paragraphs that follow, you will be given guidance as to when you should carry out these tasks in line with the phase and position of the Moon, but even this is not complete either. Once again, because it isn't mentioned, doesn't mean you should not attempt the task.

ASTROLOGICAL TIMING

In September, a good gardener will be well aware of the possibility of overnight frosts. In some cases, they will have been forecast well in advance, while at other times they do rather come from nowhere. This, then, is rather a good time to make sure you keep some old covering material available, even recent newspapers kept for just this purpose will do the trick, in most cases. Until you experience it, you do not realise how a sudden and basically simple frost can do so much damage at this time of the year.

Once the Moon begins to pass through Aries, have a quick check in respect of your overnight heating arrangements in the greenhouse and/or garden shed. If you feel it is adequate, that will be good. If it isn't, take the necessary steps to bring it up to date. The nights will begin to get a little on the cold side as the month progresses.

Curiously, the early part of September is often marked with heavy dew that may not always completely go away as the day wears on. This often leads gardeners to forget to top up water containers for the visiting wild life. Please bear this in mind and don't forget to clean and do the food containers as well.

As the Moon begins her journey through Taurus, remember to note that nectarines and peaches may still be carrying their fruits. If you have them in some sort of an enclosure and are trying to ripen things on, for as long as the temperature is around 13° or higher, they should be fine. Ripen on melons, if you have kept them in frames and pick as many apples and pears as you can, while you can. A small sowing of cauliflowers in a sheltered spot won't go amiss about now. Simply scatter the seed and cover with a very fine soil, not more than 2 centimetres in depth.

When the Moon traverses Gemini, it will pay to start work on your gutters and down pipes. You should also turn your attention to any changes you have been thinking about making. If you intend to lay concrete, extend or re-build brick fences, or even re-lay some or all of your pathways, then now is the best time to start. If you leave it too late, concrete laid now will develop holes and fall apart, should a frost occur and becomes too severe.

As the Moon moves into Cancer, look to your patio flowers and plants and start either renewing where you can, or get rid of dead or dying growths. Empty their pots and refill with fresh earth, if you are going to replace any. If not, clean the pots and store in the usual places. In the evenings it would be wise to move flowers away from window sills, because the night time temperatures can really drop at this time of the year.

Once the Moon starts to pass through Leo, there are many cleaning, clearing and disposal tasks that will need your attention. As a rule, there is no reason why the weather should not allow you to mow the lawn(s) and other grassy areas, for this will help hold back the growth a little.

Deciduous trees start to lose their leaves as autumn wears on and will then, to all appearances, seem to go to sleep until next spring. Therefore, there is no need to worry if any of your trees do seem to be in self-destruct mode because, as their leaves pour down over everything, just be grateful you cleaned all your guttering and drain areas when you did.

Next, the Moon will push on into Virgo where autumn is a reasonable time of the year to arrange to plant new trees. At this time of the year it allows them to get used to their new home. They will gain strength and have a short time to get used to things before their winter sleep. Individual trees may be planted according to the type.

Once the moon starts her journey through Libra, look through what you have in your herb garden to see what needs to be picked or even sown or planted. September is a good month in which to organise a few herbs for the garden, for indoor growing through the coming winter period. You can add to these first few suggestions as you see fit.

Gather up some strong looking samples of chives, parsley, basil and marjoram, clean off their soil as best you can. Take clean fresh pots and fill each with a mixture of ordinary fresh soil and a relatively free-draining compost mix. Put the herbs in and place them in a warm spot in the greenhouse to get them properly acclimatised to an indoor temperature. Check them at least every other day for a few weeks or so before you bring them indoors.

The Moon continues her journey and enters Scorpio when you should check apples and pears because it is getting very near their time to be picked and stored. If they come away from the tree reasonably easily then they are ready. Start to plant out new evergreen shrubs so they may gather strength for the coming winter period. Prune loganberries and rambler roses well back and continue to take cuttings from all your bedding plants that you may want to use another time.

If you can find the time, take cuttings of calceolarias and penstemons and place them in a frame in sandy soil.

Also, when you decide to clip and trim your hedgerows, make absolutely sure that all weeds that you pull, cut or remove in any other manner, are completely taken away or they will simply take root again.

Once the Moon moves into Sagittarius, make the effort to check all grease bands now for their efficacy and keep them as sticky as you can for as long as you like for you may well be surprised at how good they are at catching all manner of pests. Bring in late flowering chrysanthemums to protect them from possible snap frost attacks.

It would be wiser to not pick or harvest anything until the Moon moves into Capricorn, when you may sow cauliflower, spring cabbage, French beans and a few lettuce in frames for winter use. In the flower section, you may sow hardy annuals outdoors, annuals in the greenhouse and violets in frames

After the Moon begins to pass through Aquarius, it is time to harvest and pick fruit and vegetables wherever you can. During this exercise, pick as many of your tomatoes as you can, along with carrots and beetroot. You should now transplant any parsley you may still have from the sowings you made earlier this year in July.

And, once the Moon begins to transit Pisces, sort out your main priorities but make sure you have the time to sow some lettuce in a frame to supplement your supply through the winter period, or at least up to and including the Christmas celebrations. Spring cabbage may be planted and don't forget to prick out any red cabbages that you might have sown last month.

This is an ideal time to look ahead and put out some daffodil and narcissus bulbs, as this will give them sufficient time to settle and gain strength for next year. If you have any time left, pot on (or put in bowls) any other spring flower bulbs that you may have ready. They may be left in for a little while longer, as long as you keep an eye on the coming weather conditions in your particular area. At the first signs of frost, bring them indoors or put them into the greenhouse.

When you start to pull up weeds at this time of the year, make sure they are fully pulled out so they may be properly destroyed. Remember to correctly shelter any tender plant life, as for example perpetual-flowering carnations, that will have been outdoors throughout the summer. Check and maintain a good overnight heating arrangement in greenhouses and sheds to fight off any surprise frost.

October

LIKE MOST MONTHS, October depends quite a lot on the level of weather, in respect of what we should be able to do, or not do, at any time. There will be a noticeable drop in the overall temperatures as the month progresses; there may well be a good deal of rainfall, perhaps a tad more than usual in the north and north-west parts of the UK.

When it is all boiled down, very little actual planting or sowing really takes place this month, for it is very much a period of cleaning and maintaining what we have, rather than actually starting anything new, in the real sense. Falling leaves become quite a problem and many gardeners will need their rakes to clear away this debris.

But a good gardener knows better than to burn them. Instead, find a large barrel or something similar and cram in as much as you can manage because, by piling them in like this and leaving them for about twelve to eighteen months or so will have allowed them to have mulched down to a wonderful organic matter – leaf mould. What you can't get in the container, put in with other matter already on your compost heap.

The days seem to be getting shorter much faster and, on the last Sunday of the month at 02.00 hours, we put the clocks back one hour here in the UK. That is, of course, unless the government has decided otherwise between now (the time of writing) and then.

Having said that, we shall deal first with what we can plant or sow in each of the three fields of vegetables, fruit and flowers. We can look at alpines, herbs, lawns, hedges, trees, bushes and ponds later.

This is the last month in which one may reasonably expect any substantial growth but it is still possible to put out a few late sowings of French beans and even a few peas under cloches. Some authorities recommend the planting of spring cabbages from the August seed growing exercise so, if you feel your growths are ready, plant them along with a few winter and spring lettuce under glass. It won't hurt to put in a few more of the larger size of radish while you are at it.

Gather in the last of your runner beans – and you can use two methods here. The larger pod should be saved for immediate use, while the smaller ones should be prepared, frozen and stored for later use. If there are any others, let them turn colour as they will, then you may cut them all down and compost them later in the month. Cut remaining marrows if you have them, lift the last of your beetroot and bring indoors any remaining tomatoes.

Gather up the potatoes that are near maturity and, if you have any carrots left, it would be best to take them out now. Unless you have other special vegetables left which are not mentioned here, you ought to gather them in before the frosts arrive or the ground gets too hard to manage properly.

In among the fruit trees and bushes you need to make your final forays in respect of apples and pears. Prune peaches and cut away basal growths of raspberries and, after pruning where necessary, tie back cherries. This is also the time to prune blackberries and cut back shoots on the weaker looking growths. Once these tasks are completed, you may clear away all the debris that has mounted up, dig over soil and prepare the ground for planting gooseberries, currants and cane fruits as, when and where you want them.

In your flower beds it is time to be much more severe than you have been, for you must cut and remove all fading annuals before they become too bedraggled for anything. While colour, as such, does not have to completely disappear from your garden, you will have to lift, re-pot or remove so many different plants that there simply isn't enough space to list them all here.

However, once you have finalised what you are going to do, it will then be time to dig over all the bare patches and either re-design the garden or get all the areas ready for sowing and planting later.

If you have any alpines ready, either as seedlings or as rooted cuttings, now is the time plant them, except for anything you may have in pots, which can be kept back. But if you are tight for space in your greenhouse, shed or any room in the house where you might keep such things then put them in anyway, to gain the space back. Where herbs are concerned, you might want to take a few more cuttings of bay, rue and, for the very clever gardener, some lavender, for this is one very difficult plant with which to experiment.

A few roots of parsley lifted now with plenty of soil still attached, may be transferred and placed in a frame for winter use. Dig up some fennel for you to force later in your greenhouse. And, of course, most of the time you should always have a little mint handy so you could divide a few roots for planting or potting in a warmer place.

Lawns will need a really expert touch about now. If they are well trodden in, they need to be properly aerated either with the correct tool or with whatever you might have to hand. Grass may be allowed to grow to around no higher than 5 to 7 centimetres or so now – it won't hurt but any unsightly patches will and they should be properly repaired.

Keep off the lawn as much as you can, after you have worked over the areas that need treatment and then cover with an autumn fertiliser. If you have a flat lawn, try to ensure that the drainage arrangements will be sufficient for the coming winter period. Those that slope slightly will drain well, as a rule.

We turn now to your hedges where, if you are going to add any growth to strengthen, lengthen or divide areas, you will need to put in deciduous plants before the end of the month. Evergreens should be planted in by mid-month at the latest.

This list of tasks for October is relatively short, for not a lot happens in the sowing or planting fields. However, a lot of cleaning, clearing and tidying up does and the jobs listed here really are far from complete because most individual plants and other growths are all treated differently. Thus, this really is only a guide. All the astrological data suggested for you, to time your efforts with the phase and position of the Moon is not that complete either. Please remember, because it isn't mentioned here doesn't mean you should not carry out such tasks.

This month calls more for straightening out with only a few planting or sowing exercises and, for as long as you are careful in how or what you are cleaning at the time, you should have little trouble.

ASTROLOGICAL TIMING

Once the Moon passes into Aries, dig over all the bare patches you have created with your mini-audit of the past few days or so. Lay in plenty of manure and a few handfuls of compost and think about what and where you will put your new growths, once next year gets under way. Clean up as many of your tools as you can, clear drains, paths and driveways of fallen leaves. Keep grassy edges clean and free from weeds and other material that seems to come from nowhere these days.

Please don't forget the wildlife either – please check and top up your wild animal and bird food and water containers as much as possible.

After the Moon pushes on into Taurus, now would a good time to put out alpines that are ready either as seedlings or as rooted cuttings.

Keep back anything you may have in pots because you may be pushed for places to keep them. Should things be a tad over the top and you can't find anywhere, even indoors, then by all means put them out to free up things more. When they occur in Taurus, a Full Moon is an ideal time to pick some mushrooms, for you will find they taste absolutely beautiful when picked at the full of a Taurus moon.

Once she has passed into Gemini, you may find you have a little time on your hands because this is not an ideal time to plant or sow anything. However, there is nothing to stop you having a survey of your land and, in particular, your hedges. If you want to shorten, extend or re-shape any part of them, now is the time to start the job. You need to plant out deciduous plants by the month end, while evergreens should be put out by the end of the end of next week.

Once the Moon begins her journey through Cancer, have a good look through your fruit bushes and trees to see what has to be done. Cut away the base of your raspberries, lightly prune peaches, prune black cherries as needed and do the same for the blackberries. Tie back all fruit growths firmly and if you feel it is necessary, cut back on any of the weaker growths in this area.

Once again, as the Moon travels through Leo, weather permitting, prepare the new ground for your freshly designated fruit areas. Clean and clear away all the debris and other unwanted bits and pieces that seems to have just mounted up with precious little help from you. Remember, if any former growth of any kind that has been left lying around has the slightest sign of disease associated with it, burn it –

don't bin it.

And if you are thinking of doing anything with your pathways and drives, remember that any concrete you lay now is liable to fall foul of any early frost if it hasn't properly hardened off yet. This month, keep a wary eye and ear open for weather forecasts because to be forewarned is to be forearmed.

Once the Moon enters Virgo, make a point of gathering in all the most usable French beans you have left. Use the larger ones more or less straightaway, then cut and shape the smaller ones for freezing, any other beans you have left must either be kept for use next year or just thrown away. If you have the time, lift as many as you can of your potato crop and make careful arrangements for their storage.

After the Moon has passed into Libra, spend some time having a thorough appraisal of your herb section. You need to make up your mind one way or another, if thinking of enlarging or shrinking the size of it. While you take this time to make your mind up, take a few cuttings of bay, rue, mint and fennel. You might like to try your hand at cultivating some lavender because it really is a very hard plant to graft and grow. But you might feel like taking on the challenge.

The Moon in Scorpio allows you to take some fennel to be forced in the greenhouse. While you are here in this part of your garden, lift a few roots of parsley and put them in a frame. Remember you need to have some mint available so divide a few roots of this plant for potting on – probably in the house with winter so near.

With the Moon in Sagittarius, you may now make a point of clearing out all the weeds, remove any other herbs you have growing here and thoroughly dig over the whole area. Add a fair amount of organic matter, together with plenty of compost from your own heap. Dig it in as deep as you can and then just leave everything for the winter to do its work.

Meanwhile, once the Moon is in Capricorn, make a point of getting hold of some parsley, thyme, sage and rosemary; add this to the mint, fennel, bay and rue to make up a small indoor herb garden in your kitchen, in pots suitable for the space available. Until you can resume work on your renovated patch, you can make do with this new miniature garden.

It won't hurt if you use the time to sow a few peas under cloches. Put the seed in at about 9–10 centimetres apart and in flat bottom drills. It won't hurt either to put in a few French beans, also in cloches.

Lettuce seedlings can also be put into frames about now to help you enjoy a little bit of salad through the winter weeks. Some authorities recommend that a few spring cabbages could be put out from your exercise earlier in the year. If they look ready enough, then put them out.

The Moon in Aquarius suggests it is time to dig over remaining new areas and prepare for spring planting. Force in plenty of manure and compost before you leave the patch alone until the new year. Most lawns need to be well aerated, so allow the grass to grow to about seven centimetres or so because it won't hurt it. A few seeds sprinkled here and there will be helpful if mending any patches, which must be carefully repaired and then covered by autumn. Check out the drainage system before you leave this area, to make sure the winter won't take any toll in this respect.

A Pisces moon in October implies a check on what you may still have left of the flower garden. Colour is one thing but a close look might reveal that a rather ruthless approach may be wanted in some areas, but be selective elsewhere. Remove faded growths, deadhead where needed but wherever you do go, keep the seeds because they will be worth their weight in gold next year.

Like all years, it has been a really busy month this year, but if you still can, have one last quick look at any heather you may still have. Add to them by planting them out this week. It is a bit late for this sort of activity but your efforts might well have one or two flowering in late November or early December, well in time for Christmas.

For those of you who live in the UK, don't forget to put the clocks back (fall back) one hour on the last Sunday in the month, unless the government has decreed otherwise, of course.

November

AS THE DAYS have very definitely started to draw in and the nights are not only (seemingly) darker and longer, they are very much colder too. However, there are a few good moments because November often gives us a few rather nice warm reminders of summer days – albeit not for long. Despite this, the rainfall is usually heavy but, for as long as the rain does fall, it isn't cold enough for frost.

So, much can be and is achieved during the next few weeks but we will start with the fruit tree and bush areas. Plant new apples and pear trees and, if necessary, either remove old trees or severely prune them back. If needs be, put in supports for small or very young trees. Plant out new red currant, blackcurrant and gooseberry bushes. It is wiser to not prune peach, cherry, damson or plum trees this month.

On the vegetable scene, fresh broad beans may be sown under glass and a few lettuces may also be sown out. A few shallots wouldn't hurt about now, along with a handful or so of horse-radish roots. The adventurous gardener may also experiment with a few hardy peas – but in a sheltered position, or the frost will kill them. Lift a few parsnips and, if you have any, pick savoy cabbages. Be selective if you have any sprouts still outside that can be harvested.

In both the fruit and vegetable areas, where you either cannot do any anymore or there is no room at present, now is a good time to turn over soil before it gets too claggy for easy digging. Once a few frosts have hardened the top soil, it is quite a job to get a fork or spade into these surfaces. So, if the weather is still reasonable, these tasks will lighten your working load considerably, if carried out about now.

Try to spread some lime and a little leaf mould although, if you have no lime available at the moment, then use manure but don't use the two together, for they act against each other. When or if you do manage to dig anywhere, really go quite deep, for the more you expose the under-soil, the more there is for the elements to get at and refresh.

In the flower beds there is much that may be planted or sown out this month. Herbaceous borders may be put out and tulips for flowering around May of next year. Divide ferns and remove gladiola corms for storage, plant hyacinths under glass and pot on lily-of-the-valley. Many gardeners choose now to plant new roses because it does give them time to mature and become well established. Prick out a few sweet pea seedlings from your October exercises and pot on under glass.

There are a wide-ranging number of other flowers that gardeners will put out this month but they vary from area to area. What may be planted or sown in the south may not survive in the north, and parts of the east are far wetter than in the west. Your locale determines the way you should work in this area. However, when you are not putting out fresh stock, you should at least be preparing the beds for when you can or will be doing so.

It is important to thoroughly check over water plants, pools and ponds, for they must be looked at this month, especially where there are fallen leaves to be cleared away. Nets across the tops of all ponds are a help but they must be cleaned off regularly. While they are left there, leaves and other debris could start to rot and, if any of this passes through, to fall into the water, your fish are liable to suffer from poisoning.

A good job now would be to check over any water pumps that you may have. It isn't a particularly nice job but it doesn't take long. Curiously, this is also a very easy job to tackle, even for an amateur. Thin out reeds and water plants generally.

Alpines and rock gardens should also be looked over. You may plant small shrubs and heathers and put hardy pot plants in if you wish. Trim and deadhead where needed and remember to save the seeds because this part of the exercise alone can save the gardener quite a few pennies. Dress the rockery area with small shingle, coloured pebbles or whatever suits you.

We touched on lawns and their care last month but in November a few unsightly spots might still need to be cleared away. Incidentally, the amount of worm casts that can and often do appear overnight should not come as a surprise because, if nothing else, this tells you the soil is in good condition but the worms are spoiling the surface somewhat. Aerate the surface yet again with whatever you have to hand then use a good strong wire rake rather than the traditional metal version. Brush it all over well afterwards and the lawn will take care of itself for a while.

At this time of the year, it never hurts to completely clear out the greenhouse and give it a good clean. Grease the doors and window hinges, repair holes if there are any and make sure that, when it is all back together again, there are no nasty draughts anywhere. As you put your greenery back in, you can decide what you want to keep or throw because you never really get around to doing this while it is all in there. When it comes to having to it do water your indoor plant life sparingly.

As usual, the rather varied tasks listed here for November are far from complete because so much varies, depending on where you live. During the winter period the differences between the north, south east and west can be strong, so this really can only be a guide for this month. The astrologically based thinking for what work to do and when, really does need to be timed properly. The positions and phases of the Moon are complete but, just because it may not be mentioned, it does not mean you should not carry out such tasks.

ASTROLOGICAL TIMING

With the Moon in Aries in November, it leaves little time to turn and dig soil with reasonable ease because the earth is much softer at the moment. The longer you leave this task, the more claggy and hard to use it will become. With frost likely to become a more commonplace affair, it will firm up the ground and you and your fork or spade are going have a hard job of it.

Once you have dug over a patch and intend to leave it bare, spread lime and leaf mould over your work. If you do not have any lime, by all means use ordinary manure but don't throw any lime on later, for they are not compatible and you will (unwittingly) do quite a lot of damage without realising it.

Once the Moon has started her journey through Taurus, there is no reason why you can't put in some hardy peas in a sheltered place, well away from a possible frost attack. A few radishes, some shallots and fresh broad beans may also be sown – but under glass, of course. A few clever gardeners might even sow a few lettuces, despite the time of the year.

If you have the time, pull up a few parsnips and, if you have any, do the same with savoy cabbage. Check what you do collect in. If there are any more sprouts outside, now would be a good time to get them in as well.

Once the Moon is in Gemini, it will be time to have a fair clean out of the greenhouse. Oil where necessary, repair all those little places where cold air draughts might get in. You will have be quite judicious with what you decide to put back in. Once you have made up your mind, make a point of lightly watering everything – but very sparingly indeed. You can't afford any damage to what you are going to save and if you over do it now, heaven only knows what might happen.

When the Moon starts to travel through Cancer, have a good check over ponds, pools and any other water places. Clean away fallen leaves from the surface, unless you have spread a net over the top. In which case, clean the leaves off of that. Leaves that rot and fall through a net will give a lot of trouble to any marine life you may have and pond life could be poisoned.

Once the Moon is in Leo, complete your pool and pond checks and it won't hurt about now to give any water pumps a look-over either. It is never a really nice job but it is essential because the coming winter may not allow it later. Once you have cleaned and refreshed everything, as you replace them, take the opportunity to thin out any over-grown water plants.

One in Virgo the Moon here allows the opportunity to fulfil a short but intensive period in the flower areas of the garden. It is always a busy month here because there are so many flowers to plant or sow.

Bring in your gladiola corms to store for later, pot on lily-of-the-valley, then do the same in your herbaceous borders and put out tulips for flowering in the spring. Divide ferns and plant a few hyacinths under glass. Many choose this month to plant fresh roses which will give them time to establish and become mature. Prick out some sweet pea seedlings to pot on but they must be kept under glass or else they won't survive.

There can be quite a difference in the weather conditions between the north and south of the country about now. So, dependent on where you are located, it is up to you to choose what to do. If you don't want to put in any fresh plants now, then at least prepare the beds you will use later on.

Once the Moon has moved into Libra, November is a good month in which to plant all kinds of trees, especially deciduous, ornamental, fruit trees and bushes. If, in the back of your mind you think that there may be a possibility of moving, why not put any new tree into a very large pot where, given the right treatment it will happily grow for several years?. Then if you do move house, all you have to do is take it with you.

When planting ordinary trees, don't put what will eventually become quite a big affair too close to the house, for the roots can and will create quite severe problems to your foundations as the years wear on. In all other respects, read up the information on the particular tree(s) you are thinking of putting in because different trees enjoy different conditions.

Once in Scorpio, the Moon here signals time to look at your pond, perhaps more for the life they hold than the ponds themselves, for you looked at them quite closely a little while ago. Make a thorough check of all the surrounding plant life, as well as what actually grows or lives in the water. Make a point of cleaning the net spread across the top, so that you gather in all the debris that made it why you put it there in the first place.

After you have done all this, take the time to drain off as much water as you can and refill slowly by laying the hose across the top and leaving it all alone until the required level is reached again. You may not get this opportunity again this side of the coming winter.

As the Moon ventures into Sagittarius, try to find time to forage around in your greenhouse and completely clear everything out. Make a good check of what you removed and then decide what you want to keep or throw, and act accordingly.

Once the Moon has moved into Capricorn, it is time to turn your attention to your fruit sections. Put out new black and red-currant bushes, along with any new gooseberry plants. It is better to not try to prune peach, cherry, damson or plum trees this month.

In the vegetable area, you may put out a few more lettuce under cloches, some fresh broad beans may be sown under glass and a few horse-radish roots wouldn't go amiss about now, along with a handful or so of shallots. Some gardeners are happy to try a few hardy peas sown in a sheltered position where the frost can't get at them. Pick any savoy cabbages you may still have outside, select a few sprouts and lift a few parsnips, if you have any of them left.

Once the Moon has passed into Aquarius, have a look around at what you may have missed and make the necessary amendments. For example, you could have a gentle clean up in the alpines and heather section. Plant out a few small heathers or even a couple of small shrubs at this time of the year. One enterprising gardener I know then sprinkles a small handful of coloured pebbles and shingle in among the pathways here, which does a good job of brightening everything up.

As the Moon begins her journey through Pisces, make an appraisal of what the lawn(s) and grassy areas look like. You did (or should have done) a fair amount last month but there may be a few bits here and there that could do with a touch-up. Worm casts are likely, but this is telling you the soil is in good condition. Aerate the area well using a good wire rake; take a stiff broom to it afterwards and all your grassy areas should survive the coming winter in a reasonable condition.

There is one useful idea to consider if the weather becomes too severe for you to work outside. For example, you could bring in all your cloches and give them a good wash and clean. It is the sort of job that we often forget to do but it is well worth the effort afterwards.

It might be best to leave you to decide on what to do for the rest of the month this year but try to dig over where you can in fruit and vegetable areas, before the earth becomes too difficult to manage. If there are any frosts, they will make the ground a little too hard for you. Remember to toss in leaf mould and lime when finished. If you don't have lime, use ordinary manure but don't throw lime in later for they will work against each other.

December

THE MIDDLE OF winter is more or less upon us now and, what with the night frosts, the garden looks a tad bare when you think of what it did look like back in the middle of summer. There is very little to try to plant or sow this month and what you already have growing must be well protected from night frosts – but just precisely where to start is the main question of any day.

For those of you with fish in their ponds, it is time to take action not only against ice and snow but also ensure that the water surface is kept completely free of all debris of any kind. Clean off the surface, drain out some of the water and refill slowly by laying the hose along the side of the pond, allowing a steady flow.

Once you have refilled it, place several rubber balls of any size on the water and leave them. If or when the water should freeze, the balls will absorb the pressure and all you have to is do remove them and the small holes left become breathing spaces for the fish.

Never break any icy surface by hitting it. Either lever up from the edge or pour hot water carefully on a weak point to make the ice melt. Hitting the ice over the pond could damage the fish that, incidentally, rarely need feeding in the winter.

If you haven't already done so, now is a good time to spread a small-hole netting system across the pond to keep out fallen leaves, other unwanted debris and any large fish-eating birds like, for example, the heron. These birds are quite adventurous and will try anything to get fish but will not try to get under any netting.

We should turn our attention now to the hygiene of the soil and your everyday tools and bits and pieces that have been in use throughout the year. Everything that you might normally use needs to be thoroughly cleaned. Disinfect pots, boxes and containers that you are going to use again. Burn anything that you are going to dispose of in a bonfire but when the fire is out, rake up the ashes for spreading on the vegetable patches that you will dig over later.

This is one of the main reasons why gardeners like to rotate their crop areas. If, for example you have grown tomatoes or other vegetable in the same place all year, it is possible that the area has become infected with something that regularly attacks that plant – especially when it is always planted there.

So to plant the same growth again in the same place is often fraught with problems that you do not find out about until it is too late. To prevent this ever happening to you, dig over the plot or plots as deeply as you can. Really turn the soil over quite thoroughly. Spread a good store-bought steriliser over the area and leave it alone for at least four or five weeks.

If there is anything there. it will be dead by the time you want to use the plot again. If there should still be any vegetable waste to dispose of, simply dig it in as you turn over the plots or create trenches.

Among the flowers beds is where you can really set to and produce excellent results through taking cuttings, pruning and even having a few grafting exercises. Cut back chrysanthemums and, a little later on after you have given them a chance to recover, take a few cuttings.

Prune roses and fruit trees as you see fit. It is an old country custom or saying that fruit trees may not be looked at this at this time of the year but you may safely ignore this old saw.

Gather in a few twigs from the various trees and shrubs, bring them indoors into a warm room and you should have a colourful Christmas when the time comes.

If planting out any shrubs or ornamental trees, check out that grease-bands are in place on the older trees. Animals can be destructive at times, especially rabbits and if they attack any of your trees, take good early, and rather necessary, action against them.

Onions sown now in the greenhouse will flourish well under glass, if kept at a steady temperature at around 12° to 15° centigrade. When you venture out to select which evergreen cuttings you are going to have for Christmas decorations, use secateurs and cut away where the loss will not be obvious. You may have to be a tad savage when it comes to trimming and cutting back holly trees, bushes or hedges because somehow or other, it just grows and grows and gets quite out of hand, just when you don't need it.

You will need to continue to look after and keep your herbaceous borders clear. Dig carefully between plants and check for invasive root formations from whatever source. Tree roots tend to search continually for extra food all throughout the year and they can spread to quite a few metres away from their base. Take a sharp blade or keen edged spade and work around your border, looking for this type of root. If you do find anything, all you have to do is sever it and it will simply just rot and die in the earth.

If the weather is bad enough to stop you working out-doors, use the time to clean, sharpen, renew or replace garden tools and other appliances. Spades should always be sharpened after clearing away the dirt and rust. Blades of all sorts should be brought up to scratch and, if you know how, spend some time with your electrical bits and pieces, even if you only remove the dirt and other debris.

If you have already worked on this, you could spend time looking through your gardening manuals and magazines for a few ideas on what you could place where, or to see what is on the market that may be of some use to you.

This month, the work is going to be quite varied and not wholly complete because of whatever the weather decides to throw at us at any time. There will be the odd occasion when we could be lucky and have a summery spell of good weather, or it will choose to close in so tightly we just can't get outside to get anything done.

So, while the astrological advice given here still stands, it too can be subjected to the vagaries of the weather. Try to keep to the days and times as shown because it is important, although it may not be possible to carry out them all as indicated. Alternative days may be used in such circumstances. If you look at all the advice given elsewhere, you will soon see what you can or ought not to do at such times.

ASTROLOGICAL TIMING

We are now more or less in the middle of winter but, despite that there are still a handful of jobs to take care of always hoping that the weather allows it. Night frosts can be so severe about now that it isn't always possible to do anything in the garden until mid-morning at the earliest and then only just, in some cases. But, always assuming you have done all the right things at the right time, then life will be much easier for you.

With the Moon in Aries in December, and with fair weather conditions, it won't hurt to have a look around your garden to work out how (if at all) you are going to rotate the various areas. If you continuously grow the same types of things in the same patches each year, those places might become infected with whatever could attack that particular plant or plants, especially if such things are always there.

Thus, now would be an excellent time to take the necessary steps to prevent this happening to you. It might take a little time, but really dig over as thoroughly as you can all the plots involved and try to turn the soil as deeply as possible.

Once this heavy job is completed, spread any recommended steriliser over everything and leave it alone for at least four to six weeks. If there was anything in there, it will be well and truly dead when you come to use the area again.

Should you be unable to get outdoors, you could use the time to look over your tools and, at the very least while cleaning them all, you should renew or replace the really old or outworn items. Clean away the rust and sharpen your spades and the mower blades. If you can handle the electrical tools and appliances then by all means do so but if not, at least clean away the dirt and other debris.

Once the Moon has passed into Taurus, make what might be one of the last sorties here and get among the flower beds to see what needs to be cut away, pruned or, possibly grafted. Cut back the chrysanthemums and prune a few of the roses that may have got out of hand. There is a very old country saying "Prune roses and fruit trees as you see fit." This refers to almost any time of the year but not in December. What has to be done, must be done.

Once the Moon is hosted by Gemini, have a good look around the garden and collect all the twigs from the various trees and bushes that you might want to use as indoor decorations for the coming festive season. They often look much better than shop bought versions and are just as easily disposed of afterward.

As the Moon moves into Cancer, have a check over pools, ponds and other water features. Frost and snow can wreak havoc here and the damage is so often nearly irreparable. Clear away any of the usual debris, sweep (if possible) snow away and, if needs be, clean and drain some of the water away and refill slowly.

A couple of rubber balls of any size should be left on the surface so that, if the water freezes, they will absorb the increased pressure. All you have to do is take them out and the small holes left become little breathing areas.

Never break ice on any water surface by hitting it – you could damage the animal life. Pour hot water on to the ice or leave a small log or a tree branch half in and half out of the water, so all that you have to do is lift. As the ice breaks underneath, remove some of it and lay the log or branch back again, ready for another time.

When Leo has the Moon passing through it, renew or refresh the grease bands where needed on all your trees. One way or another, all the animal life that visits your garden can be quite destructive, especially the rabbit.

Making this effort now will save a lot of time and trouble early next year. If you have any time left over from this, or the weather is that inhospitable, have a read through whatever magazines you may have, for there might be one or two very useful tips you could adopt later on.

With the Moon in Libra, you may now cut and trim holly bushes and hedges and, while looking at your trees check them over for invasive root growths because these formations can spread for up to quite a few metres away. The easiest, and best way, to deal with this is to get a sharp saw or blade and sever them completely. A sharp-edged shovel will sever any offending roots as a rule.

As the Moon edges into Sagittarius it will give you the opportunity to be a tad adventurous and put out a few onions under glass but they must be kept at around 12° to 15° centigrade if they are to survive. Take up a few roots of mint and put them into one of your greenhouse frames. Once they start to shoot, you can use them as you see fit.

Now would be a good time to clean off any moss growths on paths. A solution of ordinary household bleach will be helpful here. Spray it on, leave it for about half-an-hour or so and then clean it off with a scrubbing brush or a besom broom.

The Moon in Capricorn gives the help you might want to prepare for sowing seeds in the greenhouse at a later time. Really clean out all your old boxes, pots and other containers and make sure they are free from any possible infection. Put in soil, sand, peat and lime to suit and make sure your frame(s) will be ready for this exercise once you can or should start. You could also arrange for deliveries of lime, peat, sand and other materials to be delivered. If you have one, give your warm frame a quick once-over.

Once the Moon enters Aquarius, check all wooden trellis work, wooden fences and any part of a patio construction made from wood. It is time now to use as much preservative as needed to treat these areas properly, before it becomes too late. It wasn't that long ago most of us would use creosote but this is now very hard to get – if at all. There are a few reasonable substitutes around or there are many alternatives, all of which will do the job and most won't harm any nearby plant life.

Put a couple of hours in among your flower areas that are still producing and take a few cuttings, prune and make a few grafting arrangements where you want them. You could cut back on your chrysanthemums and, after they have had a chance to recover, take a few cuttings. Prune grape vines under glass where needed. Continue to prune rose and fruit growths, where applicable.

With the Moon in Pisces, and if you have the time to do so, move around the various areas in your garden to make one last attempt at winter preparations where you think necessary – just in case it gets really severe. Clean the netting on the pond and the surface once more, if it is possible to do so. Sweep the lawn and grassy areas with a besom broom. Sprinkle anti-frost salt on car drives or other walkways and pathways.

One other task, often forgotten, is to remember to wrap insulation around all garden taps. There are special products on the market to protect this water supply. However, if you can, turn off the water supply to outside water taps to avoid the damage a burst pipe can wreak.

Milton Keynes UK
Ingram Content Group UK Ltd.
UKHW022038310823
427823UK00014B/371